latin jazz

contents

ISBN 978-0-634-01775-9

HAL•LEONARD®

7777 W. BLUEMOUND RD. P.O. BOX 13819 MILWAUKEE, WI 53213

Visit Hal Leonard Online at
www.halleonard.com

ADIÓS

English Words by EDDIE WOODS
Spanish Translation and Music by ENRIC MADRIGUERA

Freely

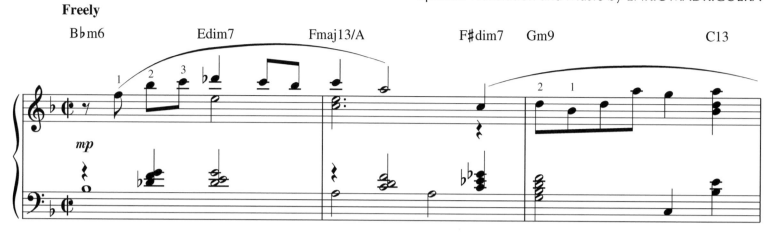

Playful Latin feel

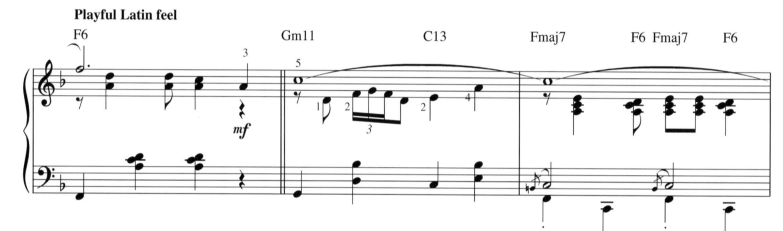

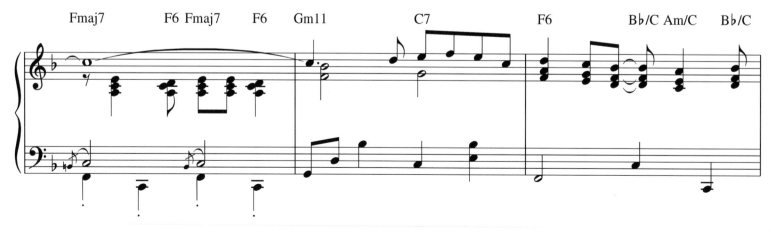

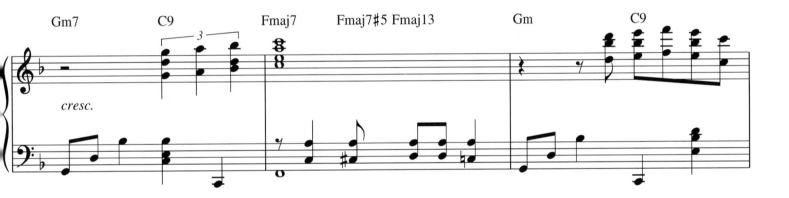

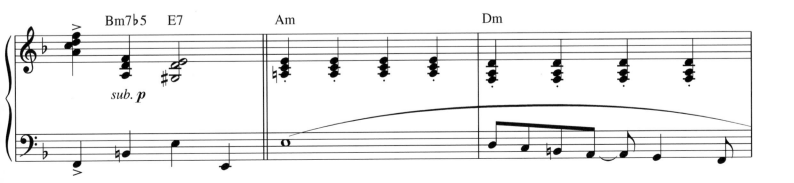

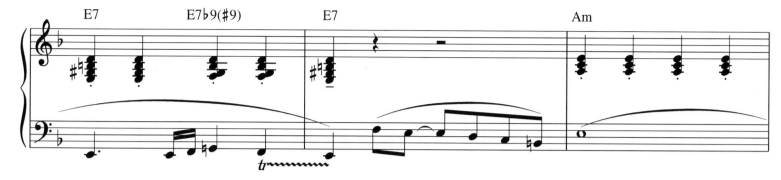

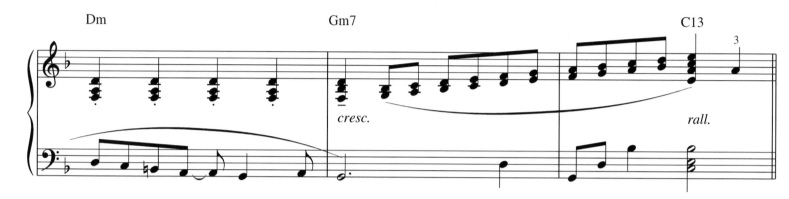

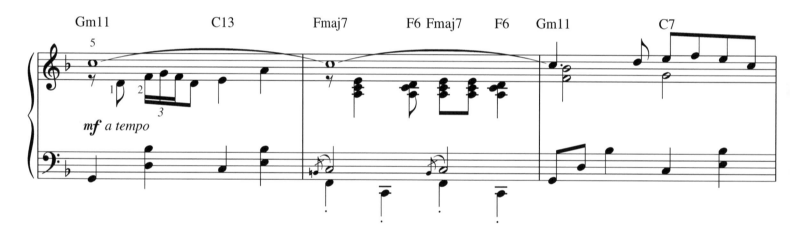

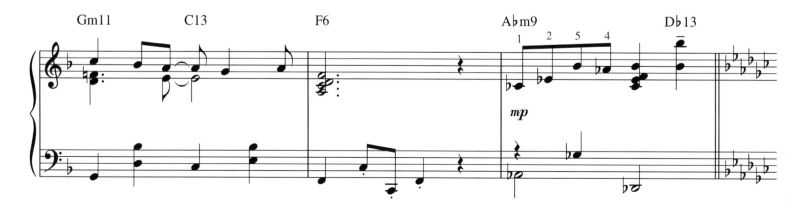

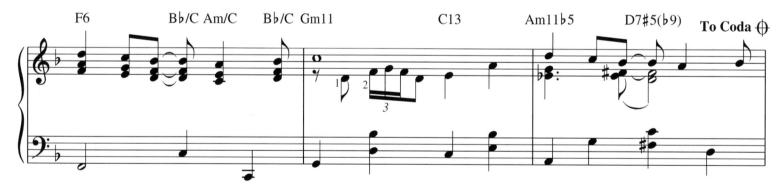

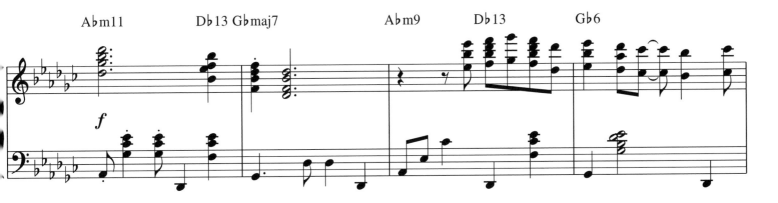

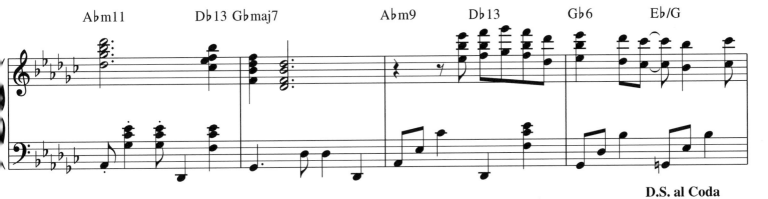

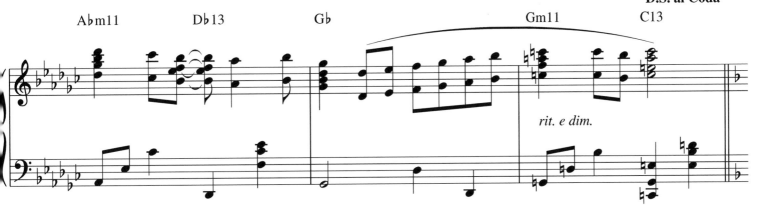

D.S. al Coda

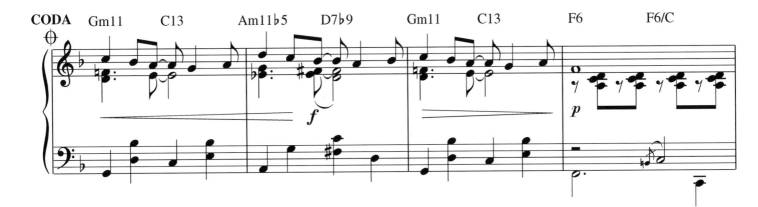

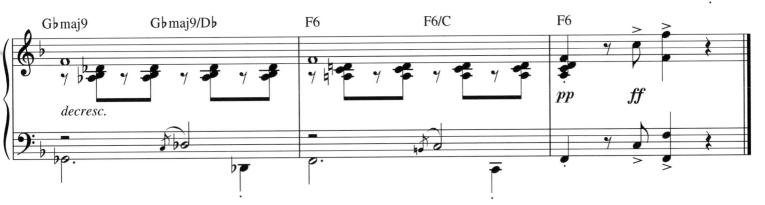

AFRO BLUE

By MONGO SANTAMARIA

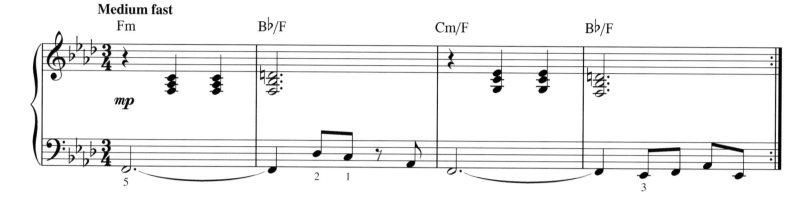

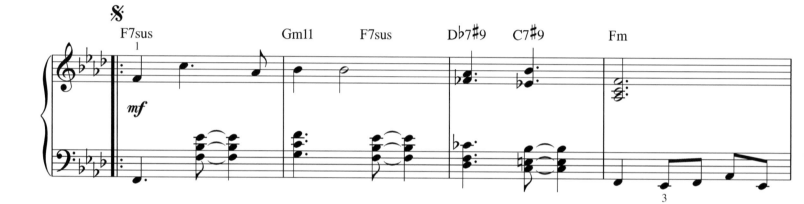

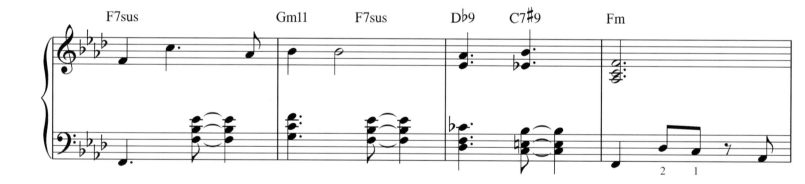

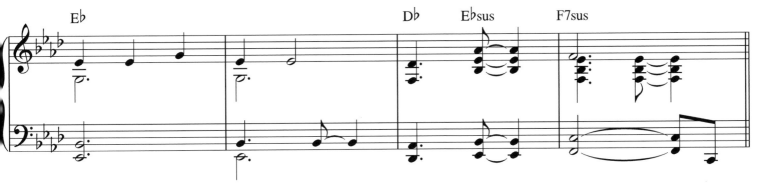

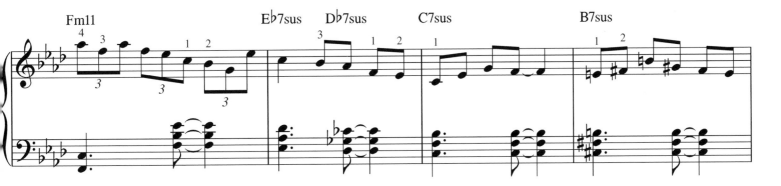

8

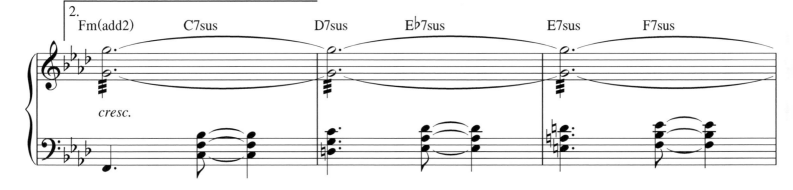

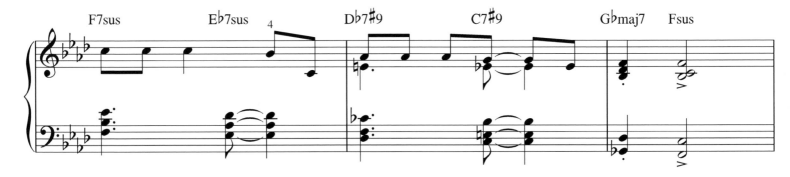

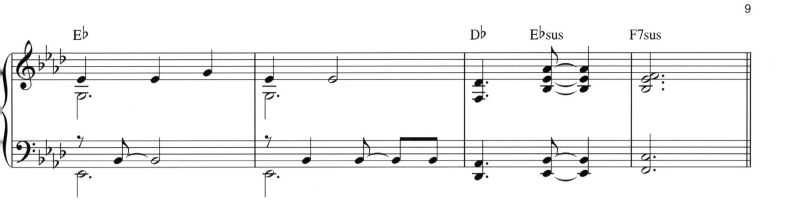

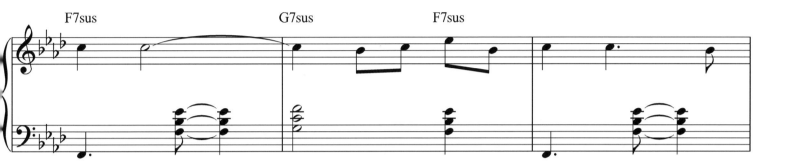

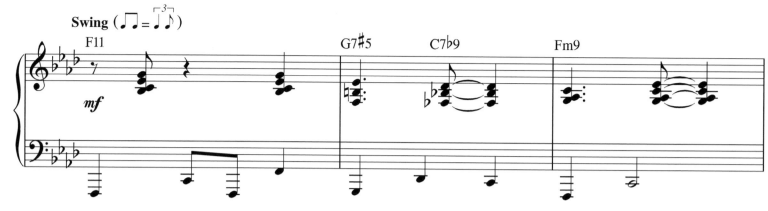

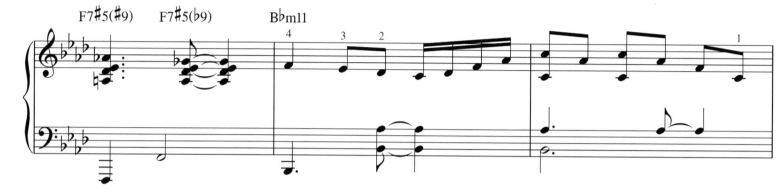

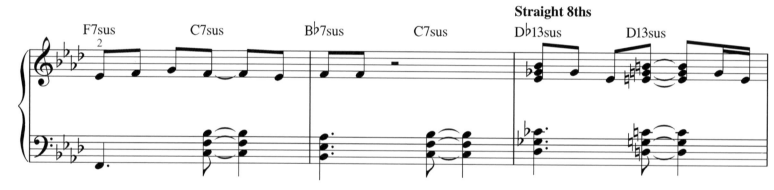

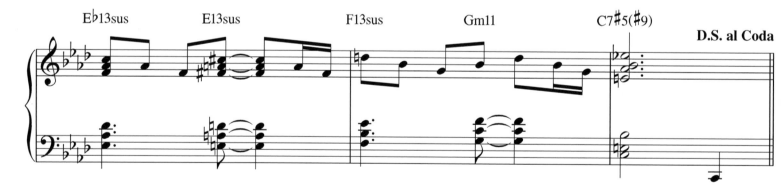

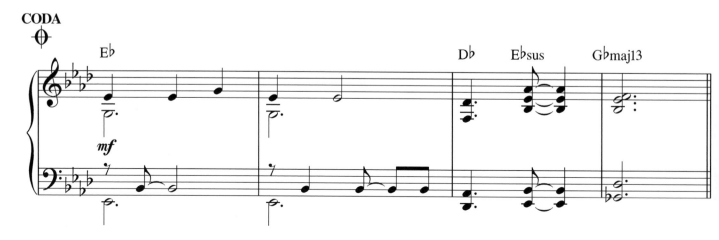

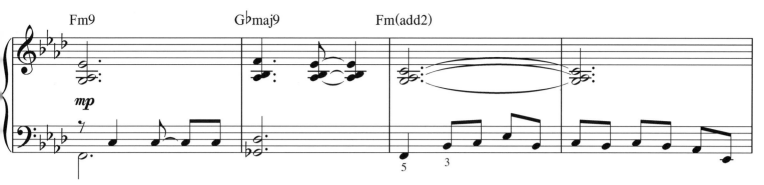

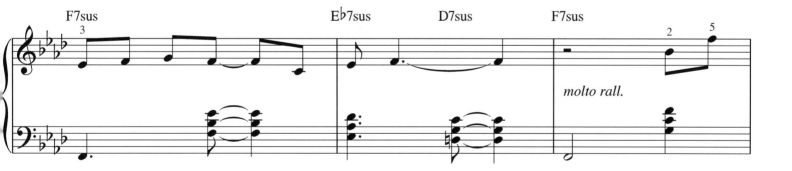

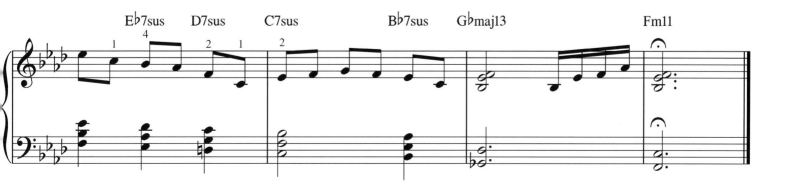

BRAZIL

Original Words and Music by ARY BARROSO
English Lyrics by S.K. RUSSELL

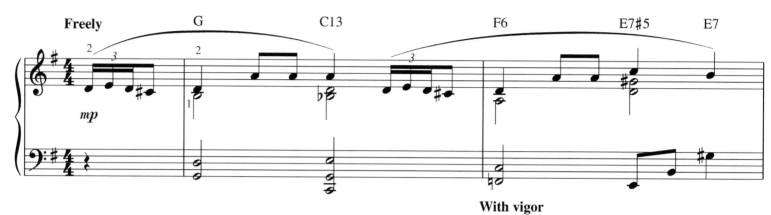

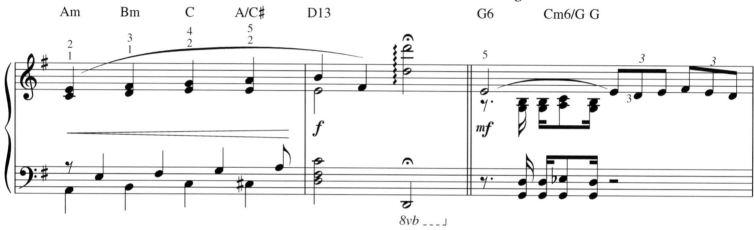

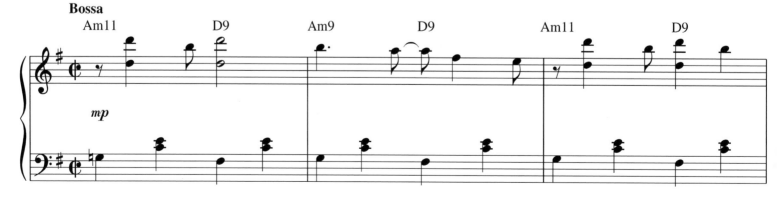

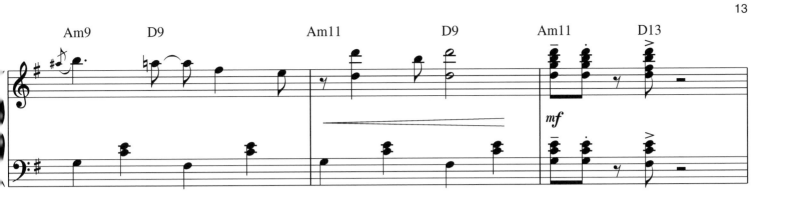

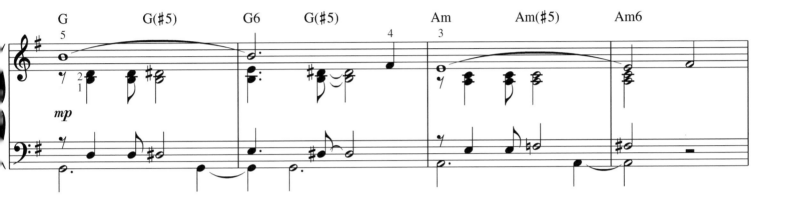

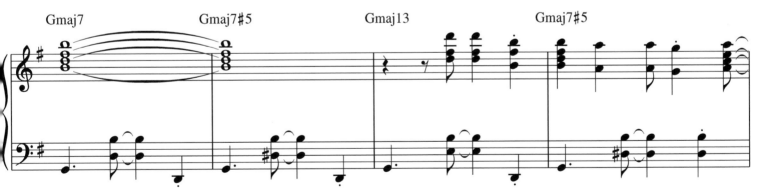

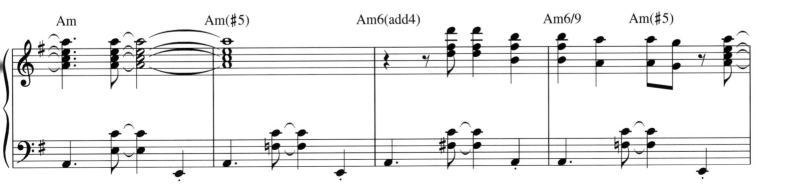

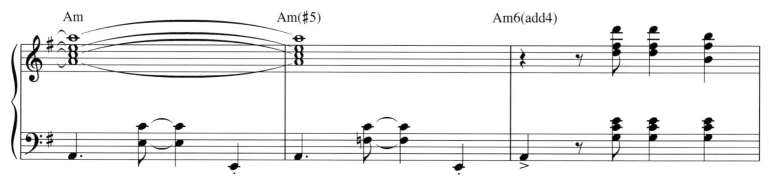

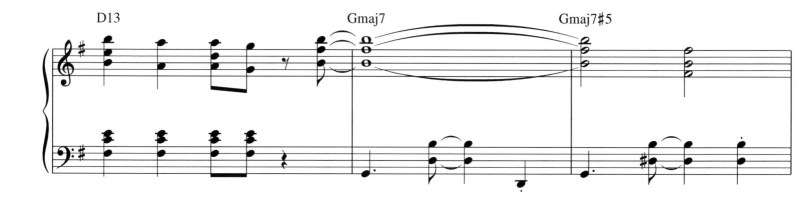

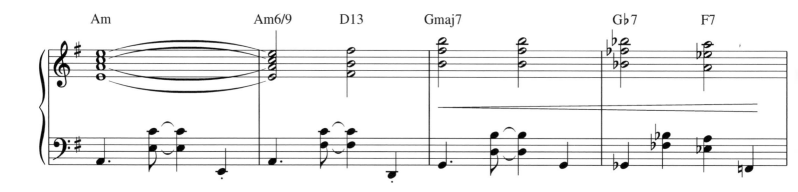

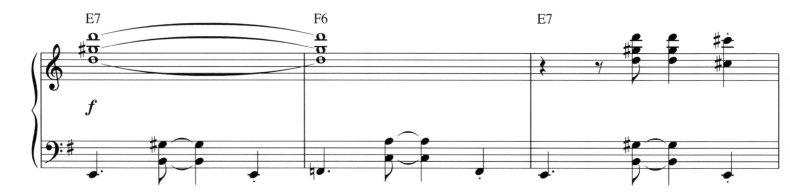

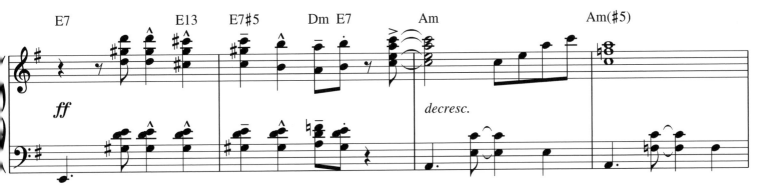

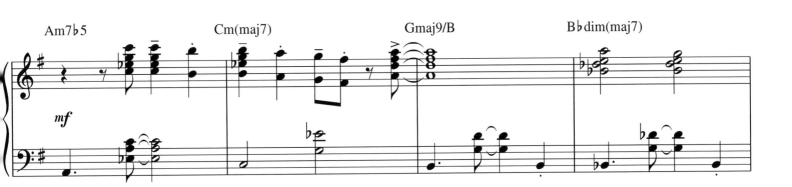

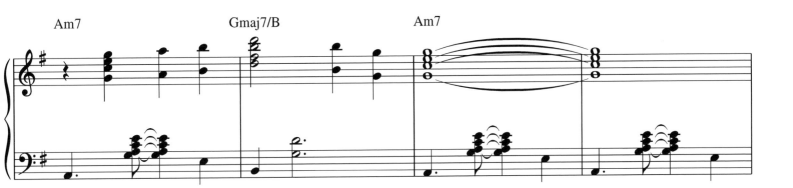

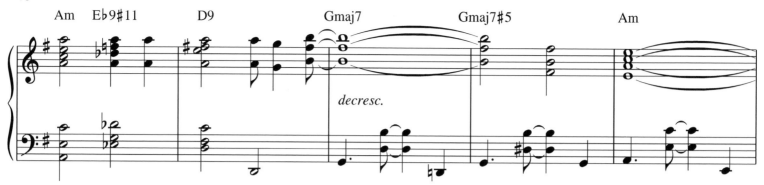

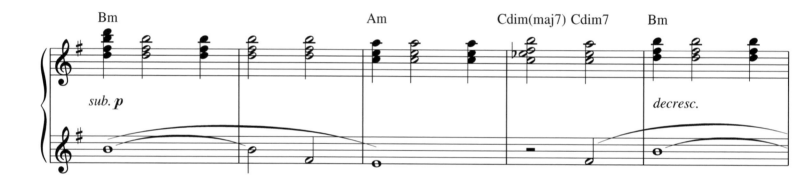

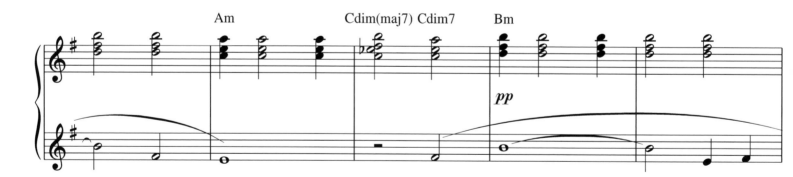

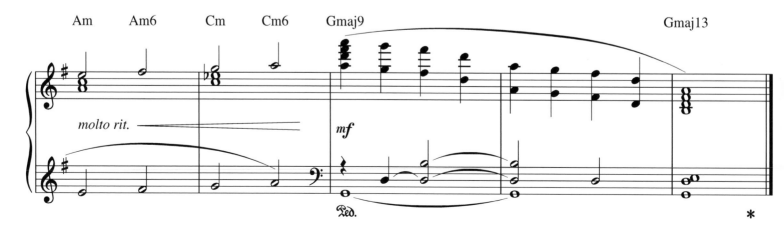

CHEGA DE SAUDADE
(No More Blues)

Original Text by VINICIUS DE MORAES
Music by ANTONIO CARLOS JOBIM

Bright Samba

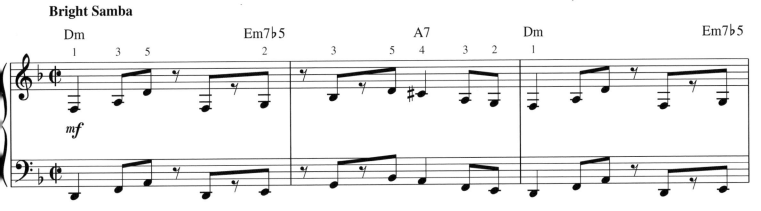

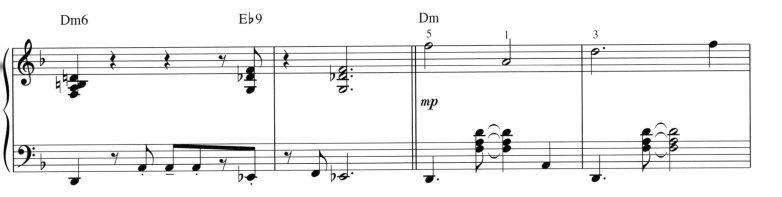

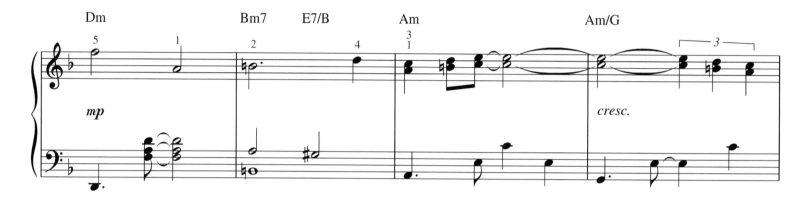

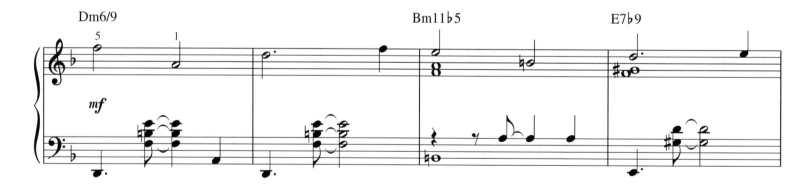

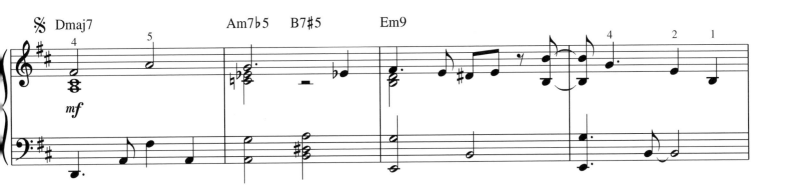

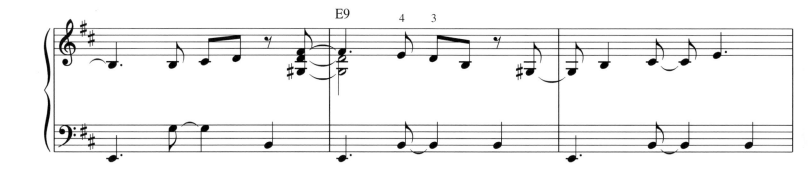

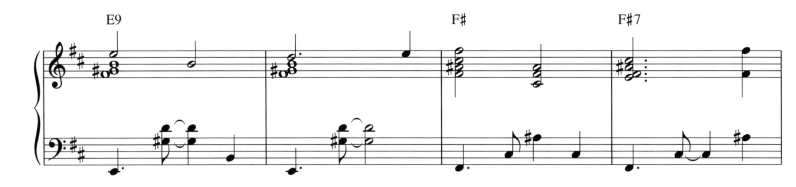

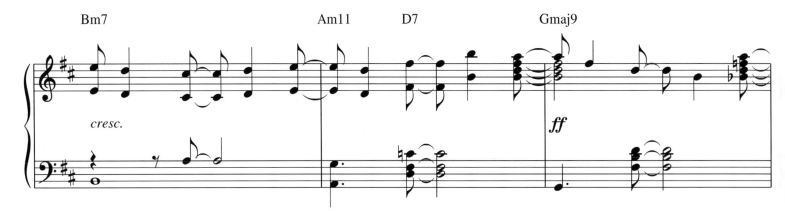

To Coda ⊕

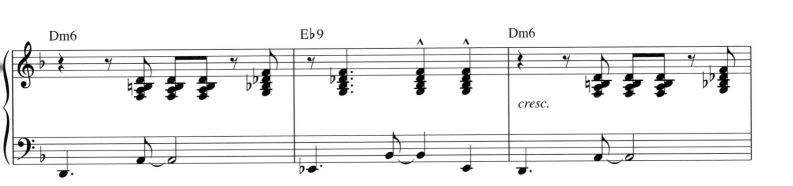

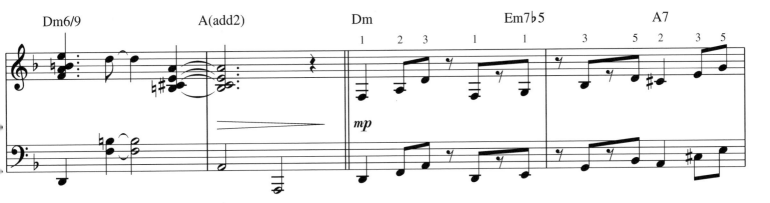

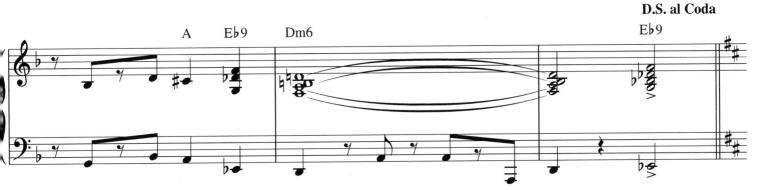

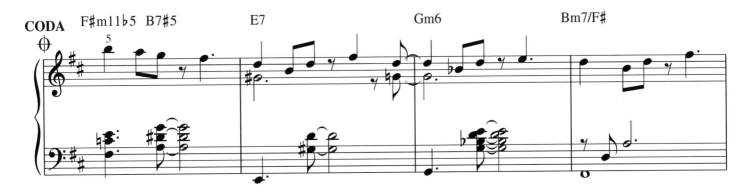

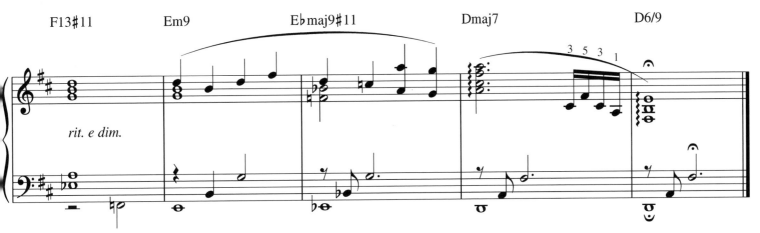

A DAY IN THE LIFE OF A FOOL
(Manhã de Carnaval)

By LUIZ BONFA

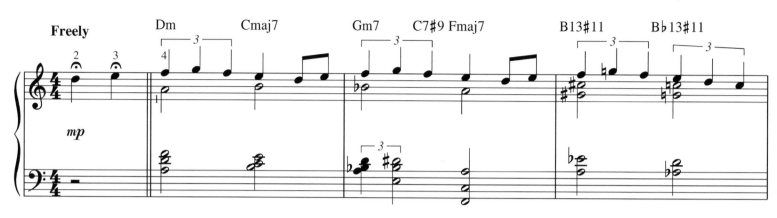

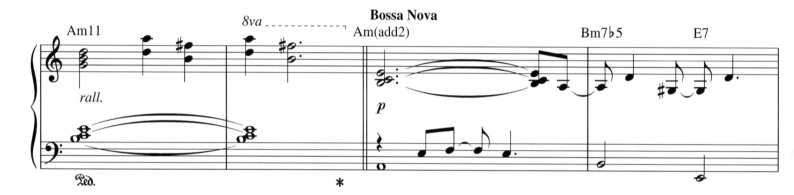

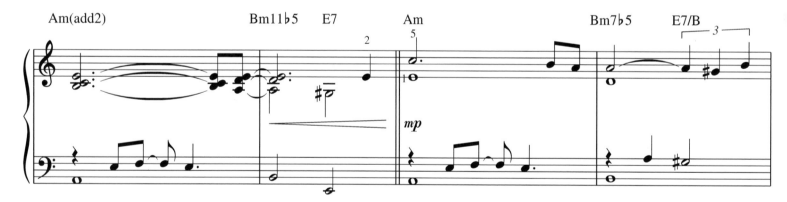

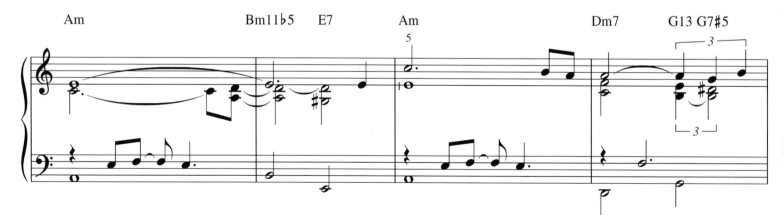

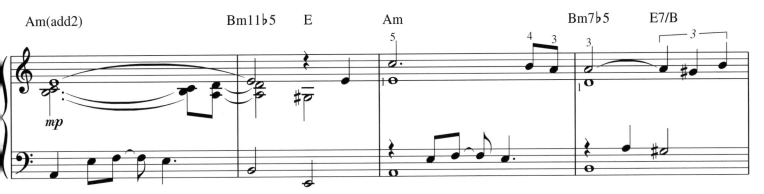
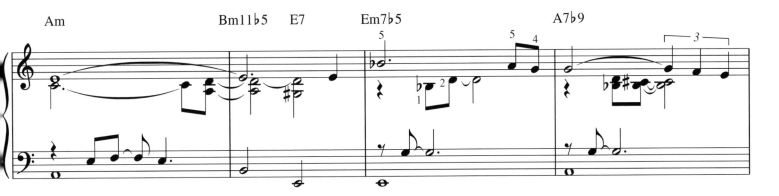

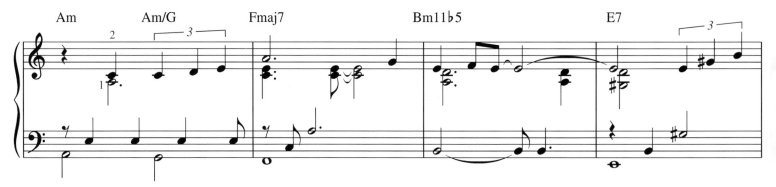

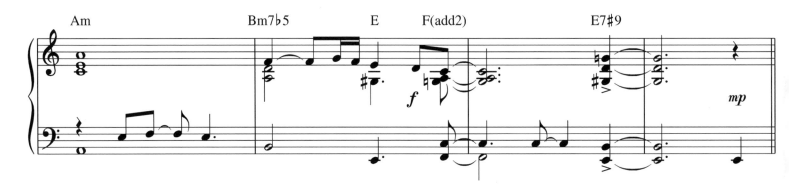

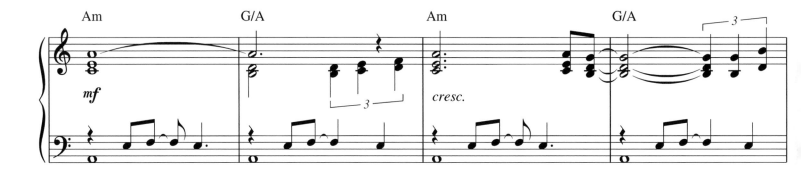

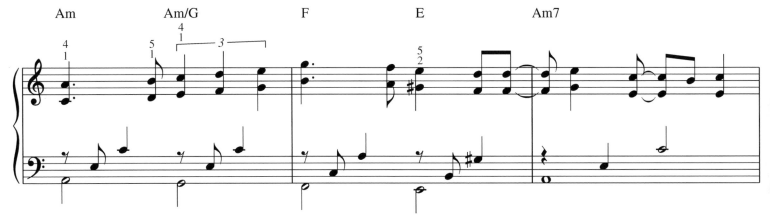

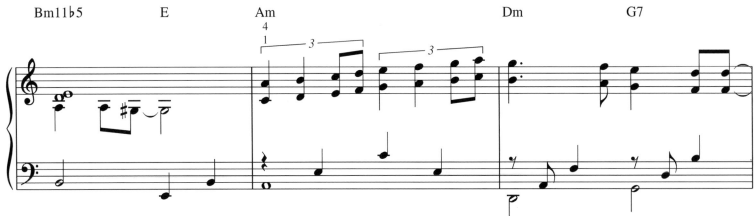

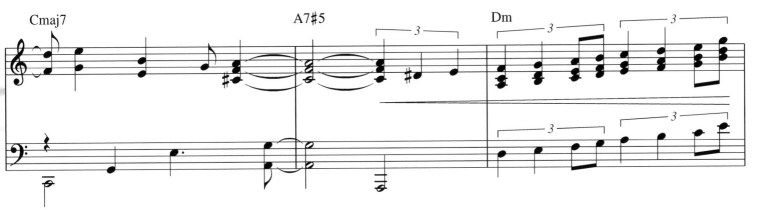

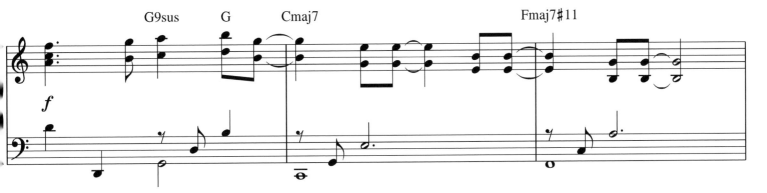

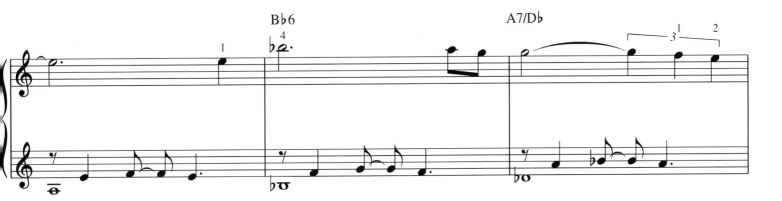

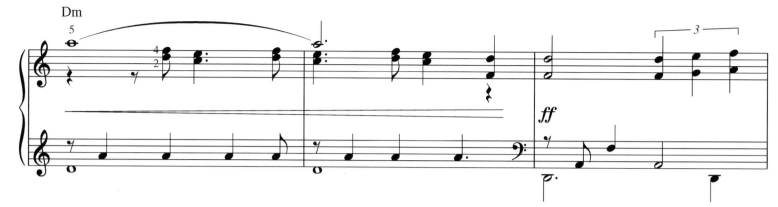

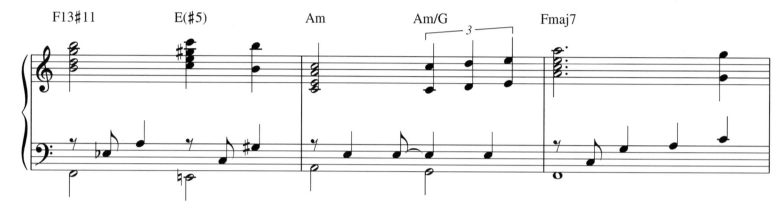

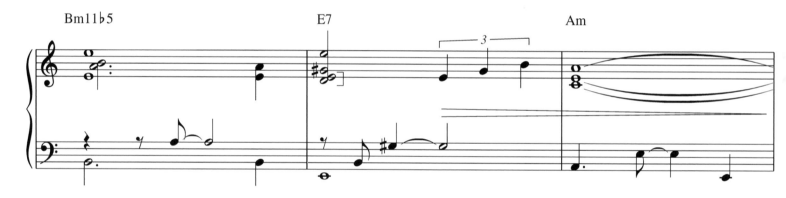

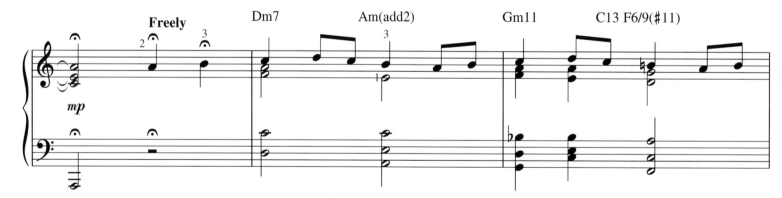

FRENESÍ

Words and Music by
ALBERTO DOMINGUEZ

Moderate Latin

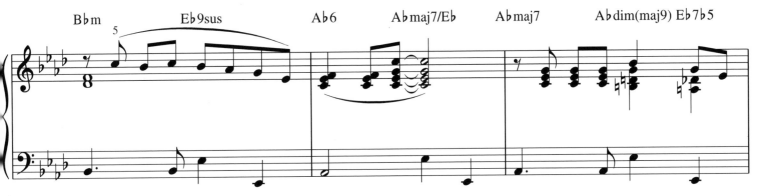

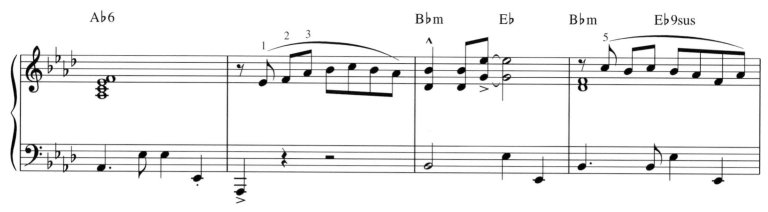

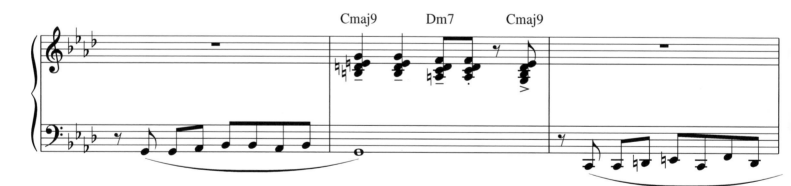

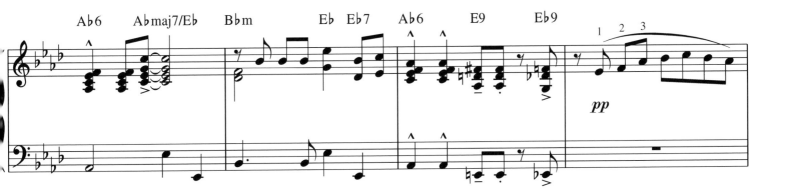

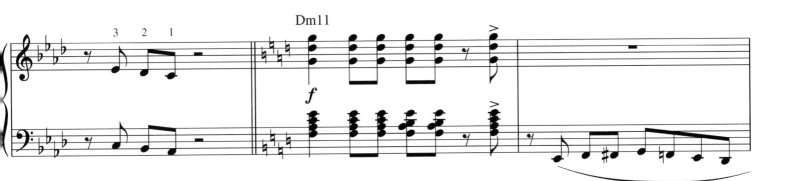

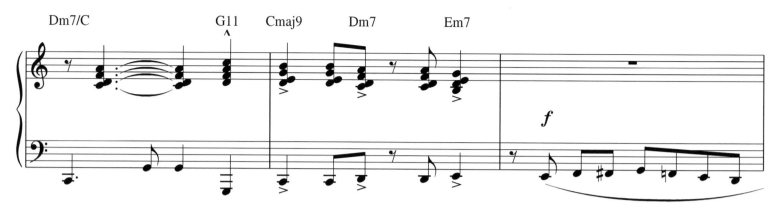

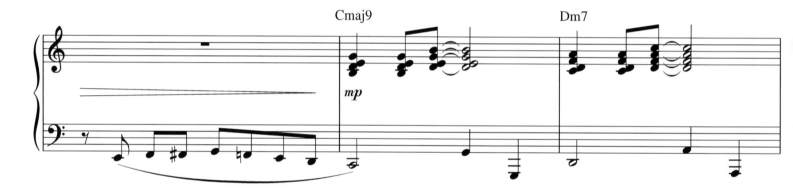

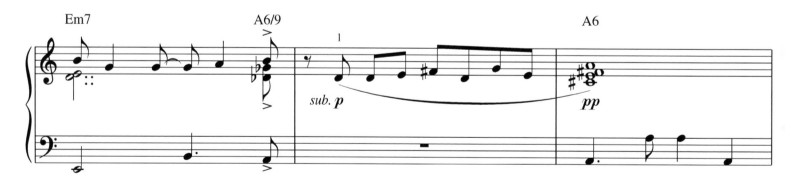

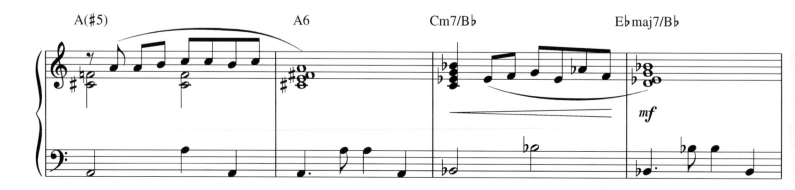

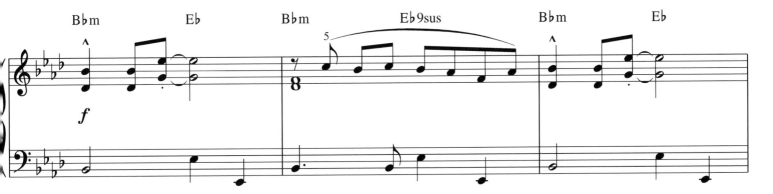

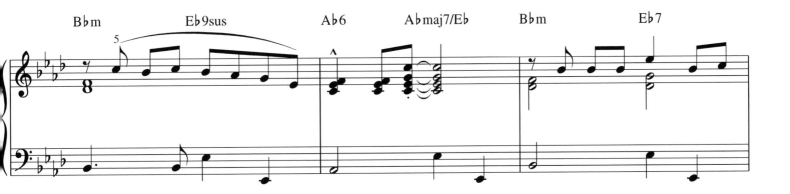

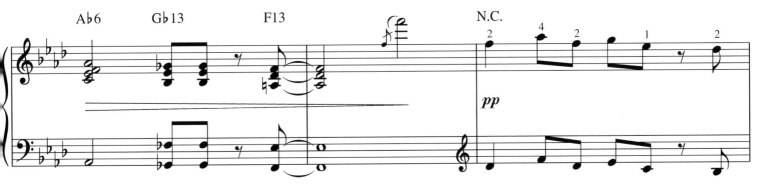

DESAFINADO

Original Text by NEWTON MENDONCA
Music by ANTONIO CARLOS JOBIM

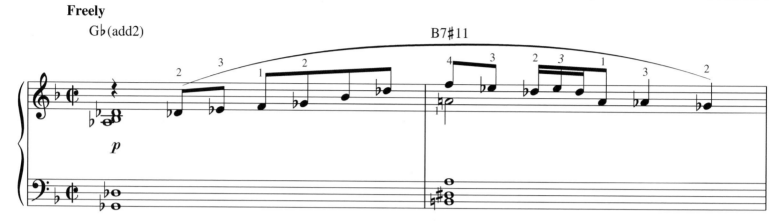

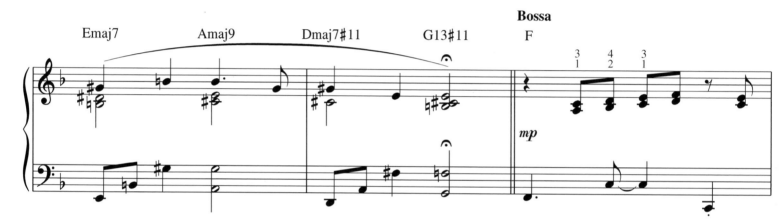

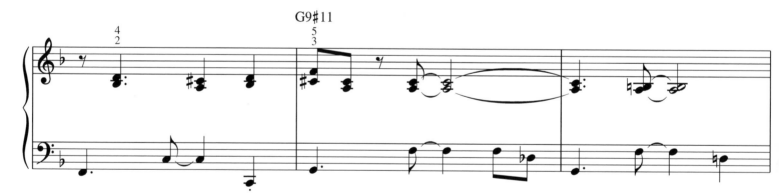

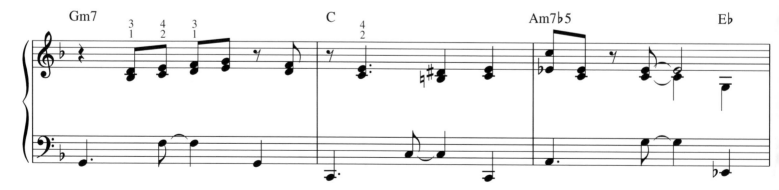

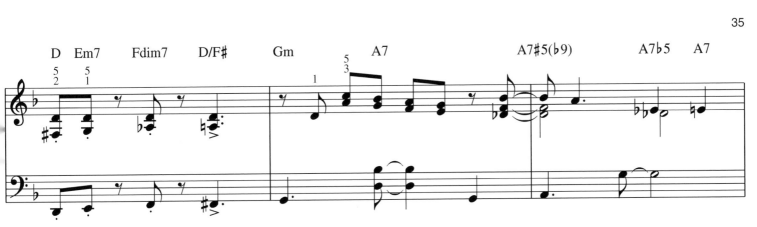

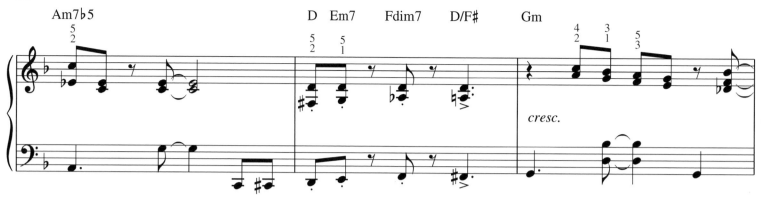

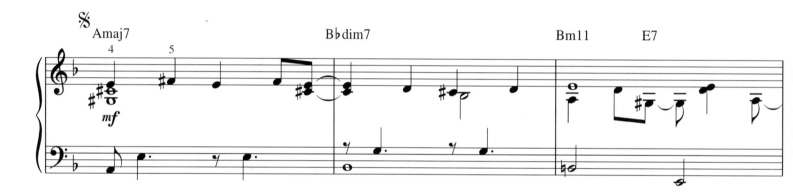

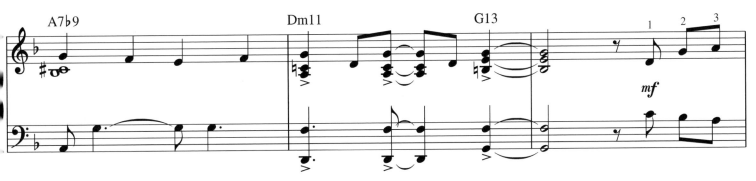

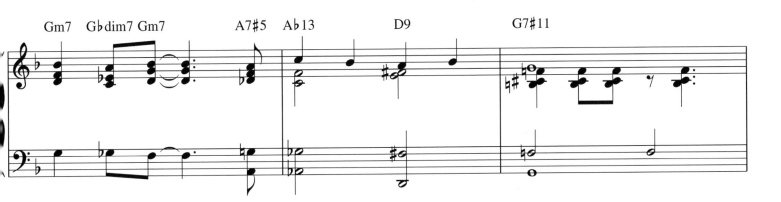

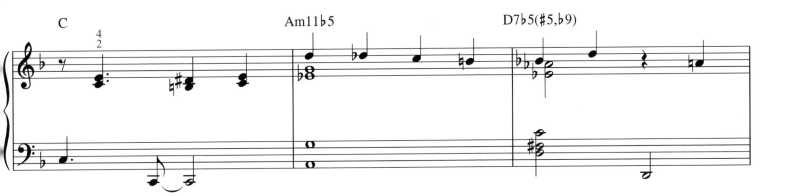

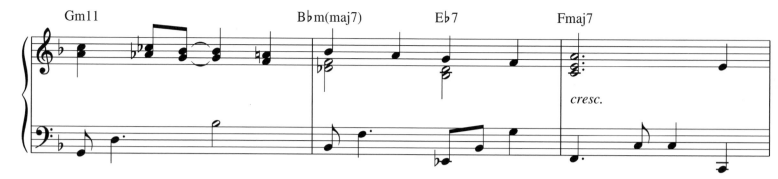

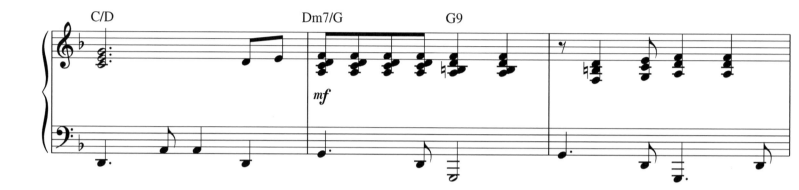

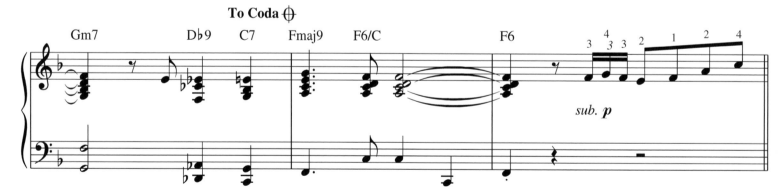

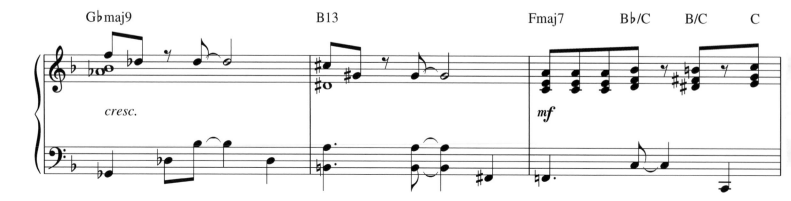

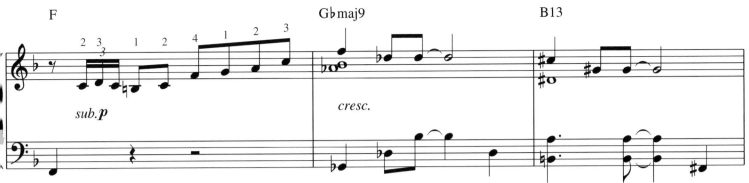

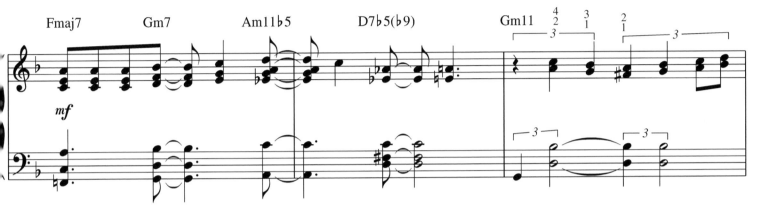

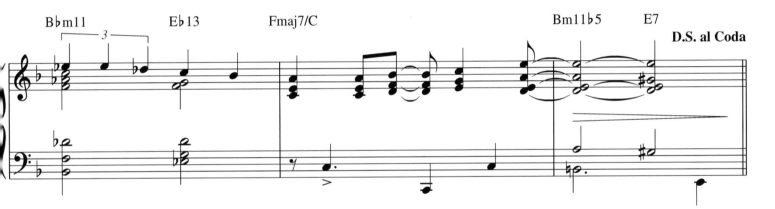

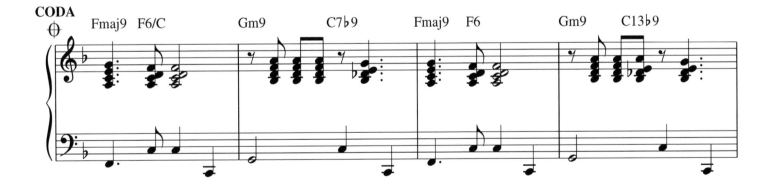

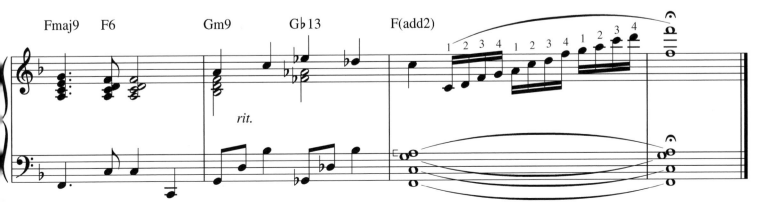

DINDI

Music by ANTONIO CARLOS JOBIM
Portuguese Lyrics by ALOYSIO DE OLIVEIRA
English Lyrics by RAY GILBERT

Gently

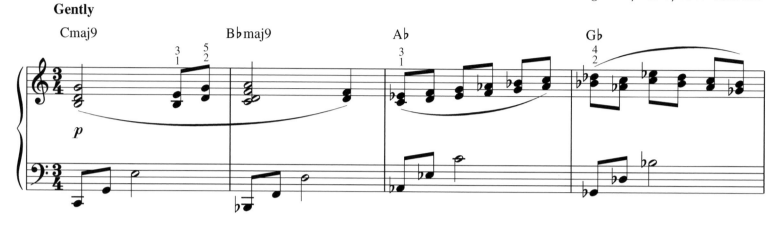

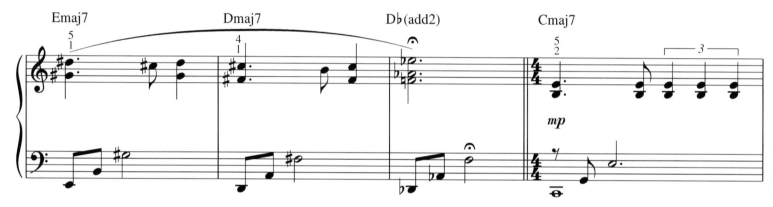

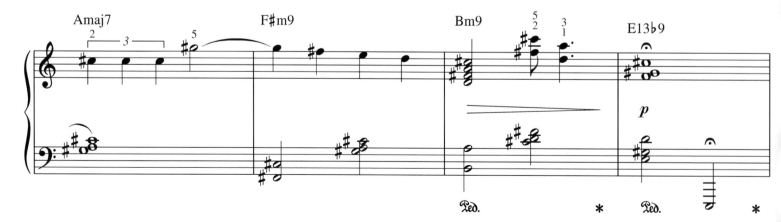

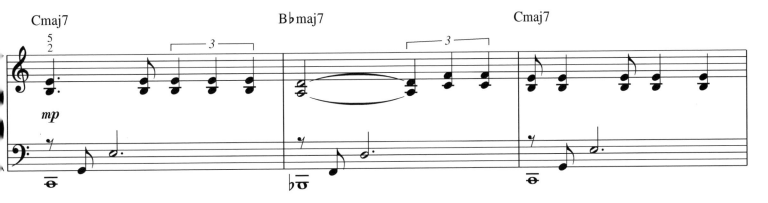

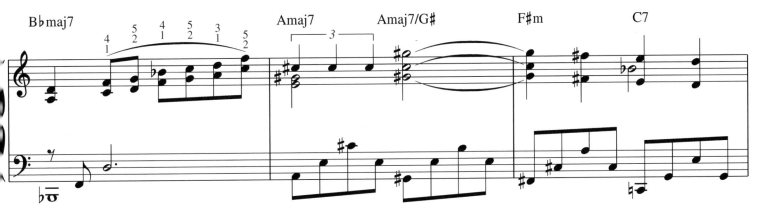

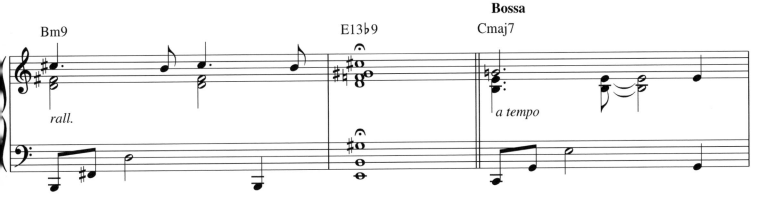

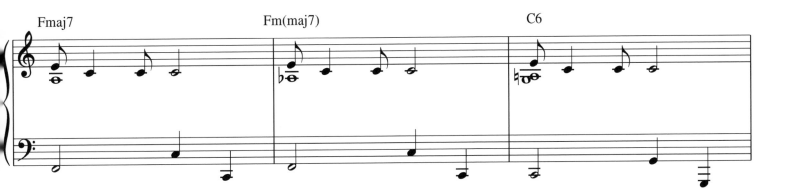

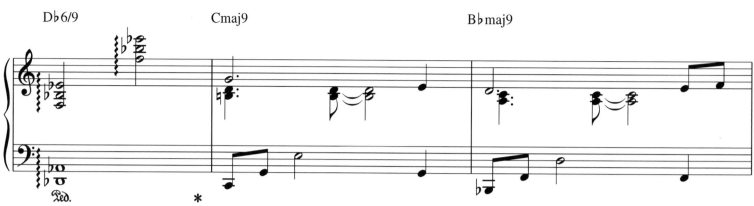

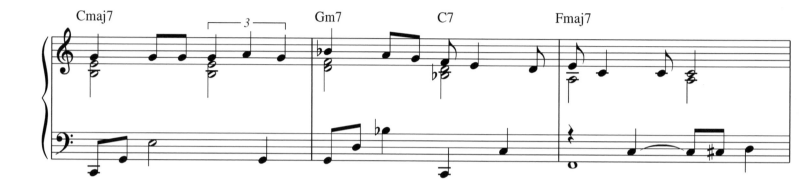

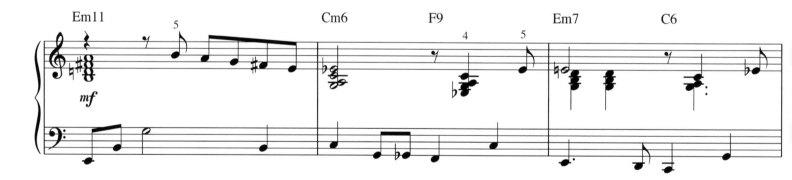

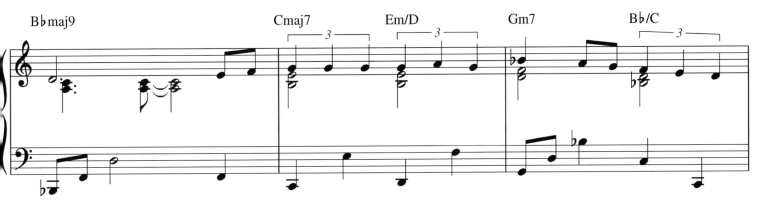

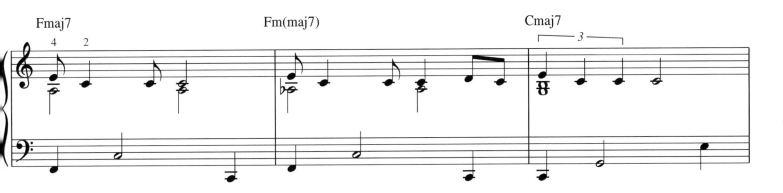

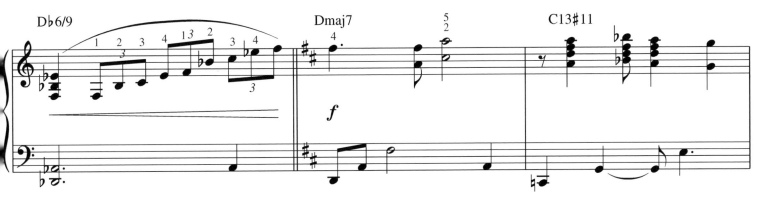

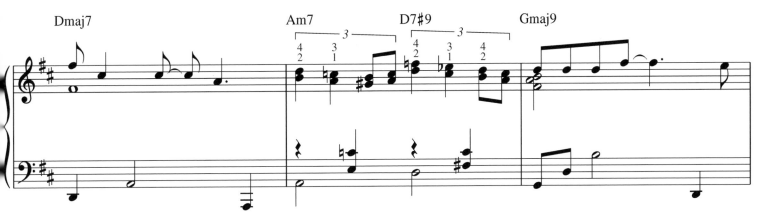

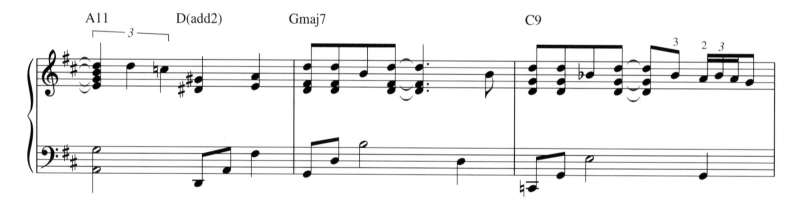

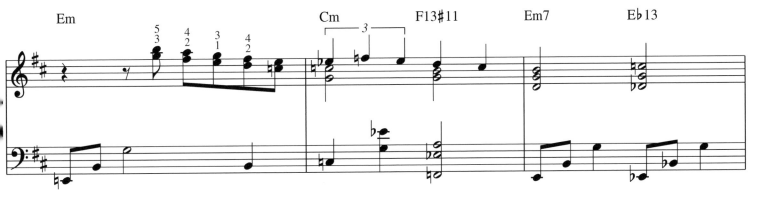

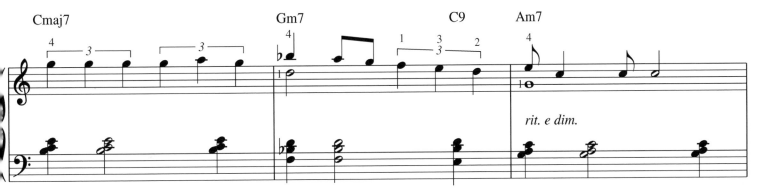

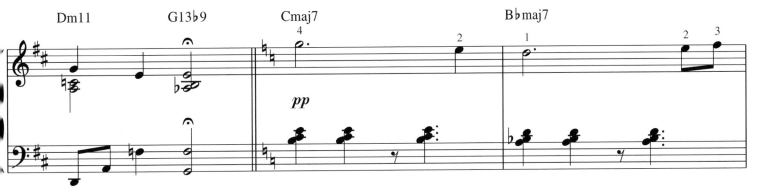

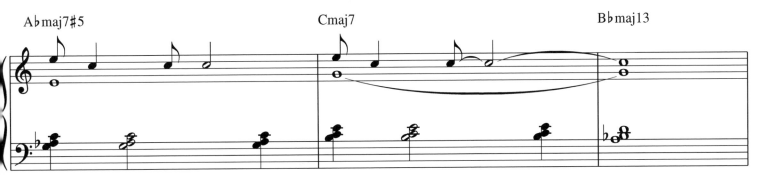

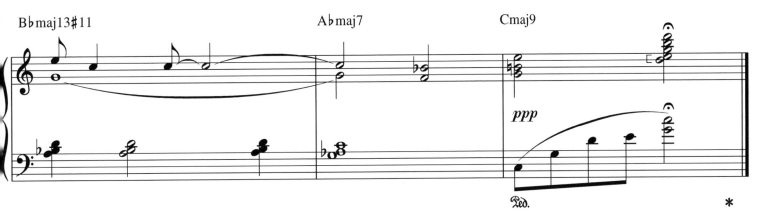

THE GIFT!
(Recado Bossa Nova)

Music by DJALMA FERREIRA
Original Lyric by LUIZ ANTONIO
English Lyric by PAUL FRANCIS WEBSTER

Bright Bossa

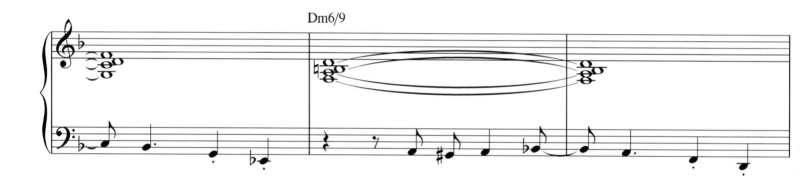

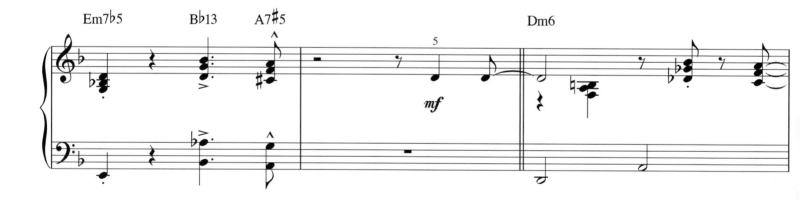

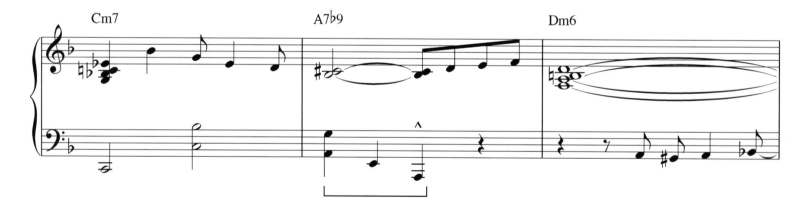

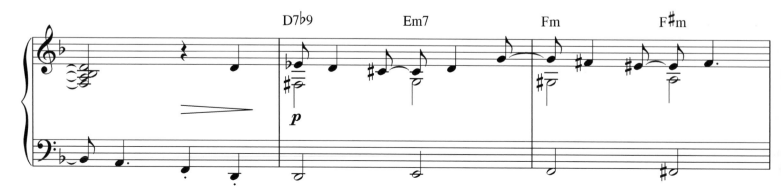

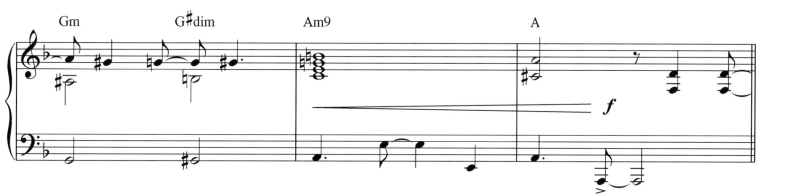

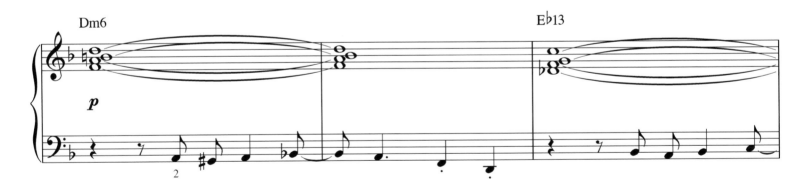

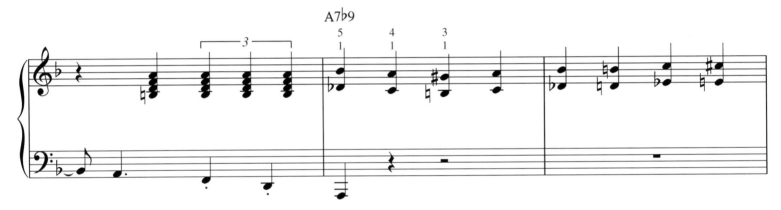

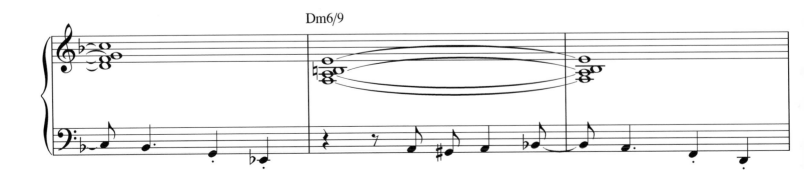

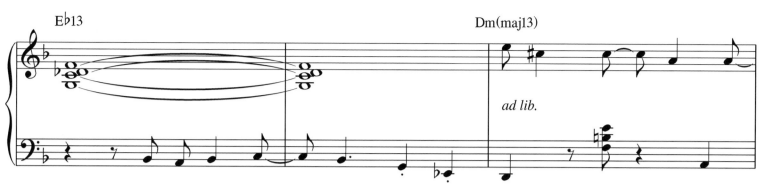

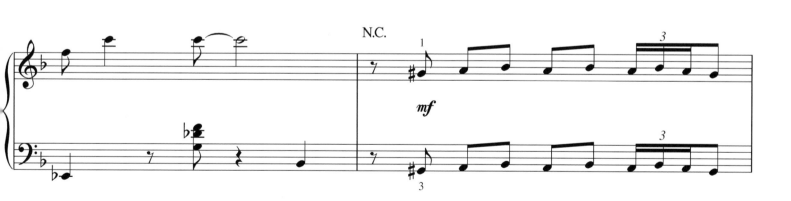

MAMBO JAMBO
(Que Rico el Mambo)

English Words by RAYMOND KARL and CHARLIE TOWNE
Original Words and Music by DAMASO PÉREZ PRADO

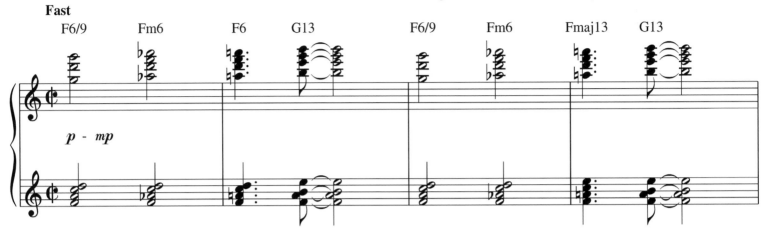

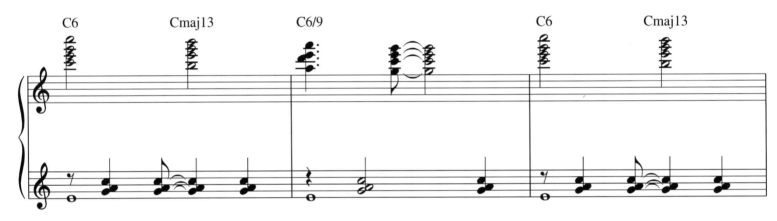

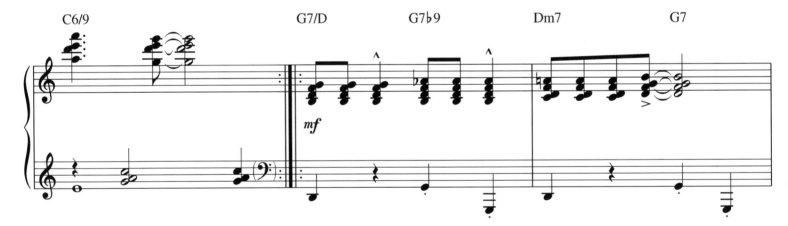

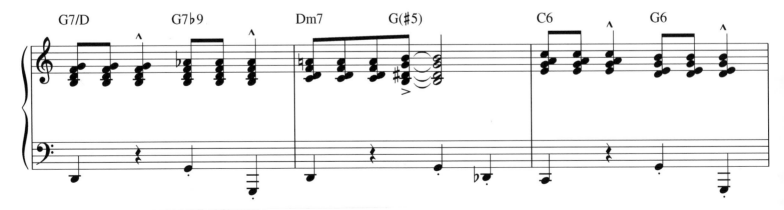

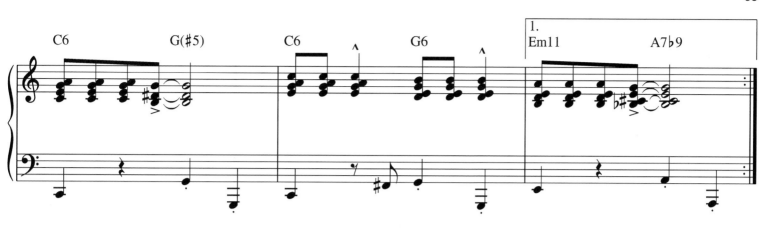

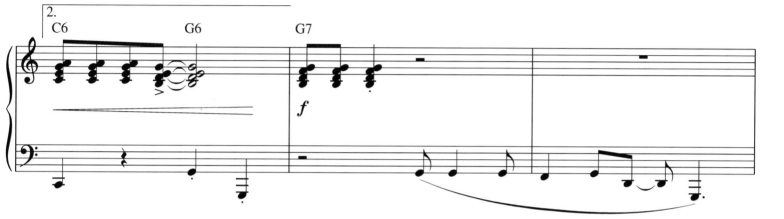

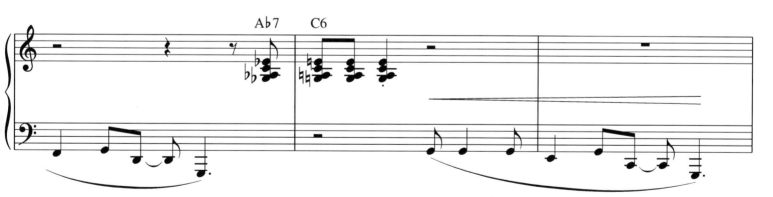

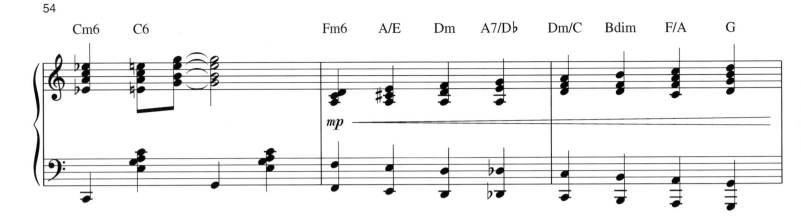

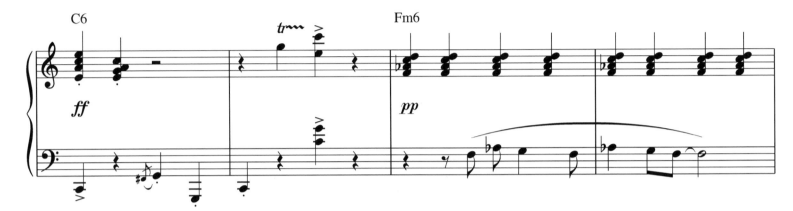

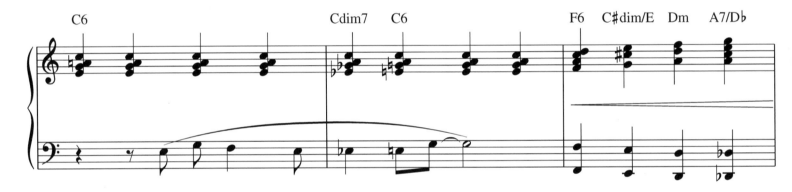

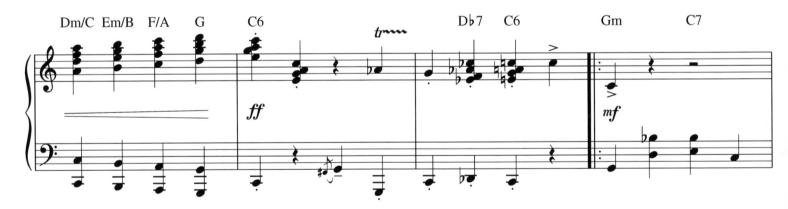

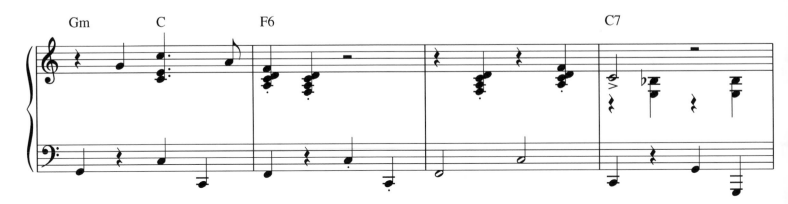

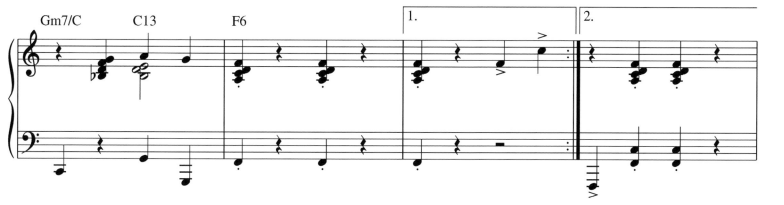

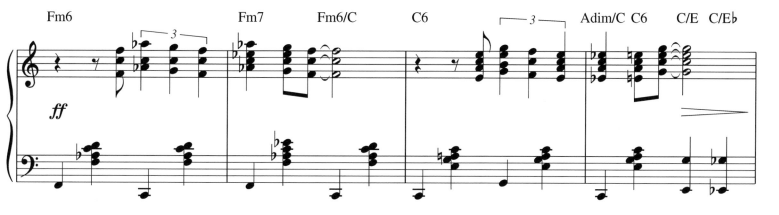

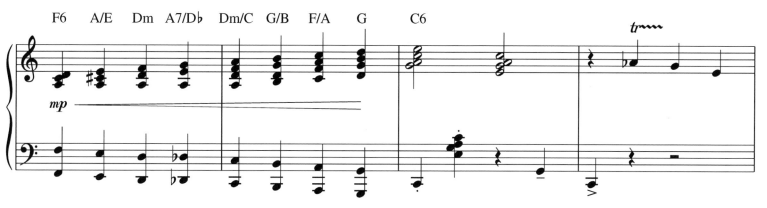

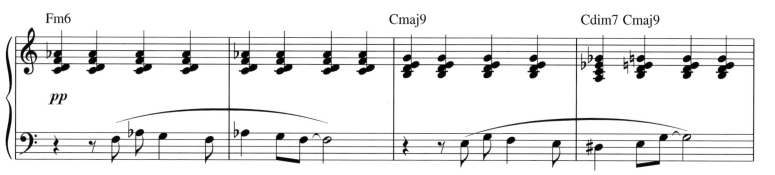

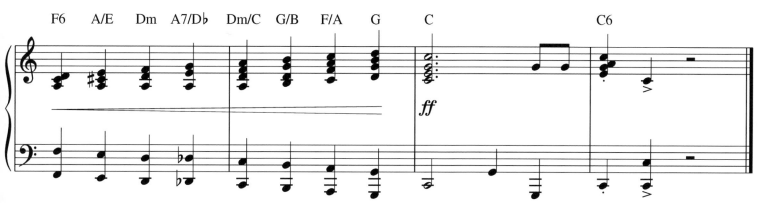

MAMBO #5

Words and Music by
DAMASO PÉREZ PRADO

Bright Mambo

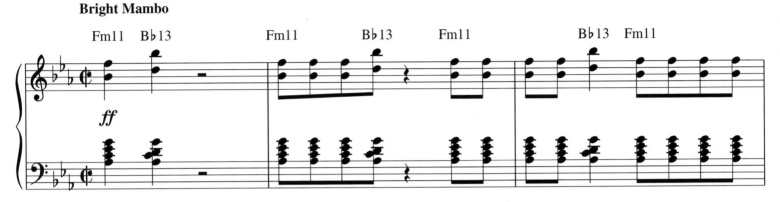

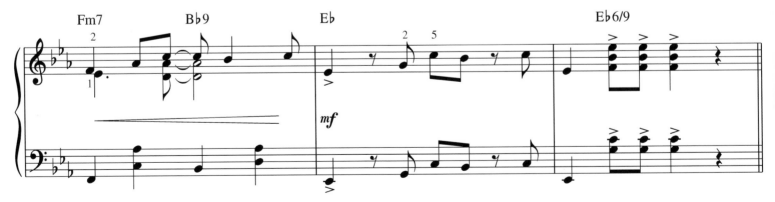

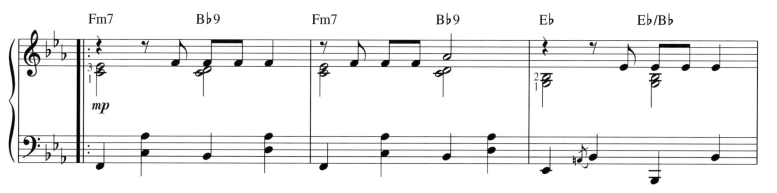

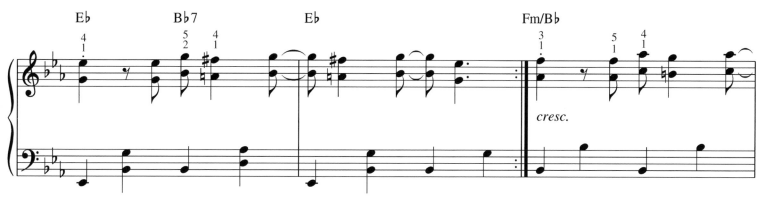

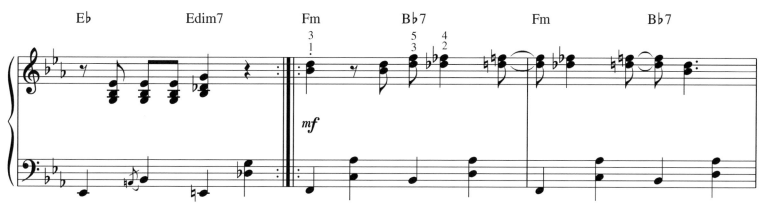

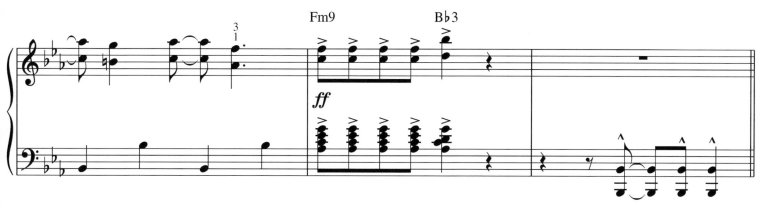

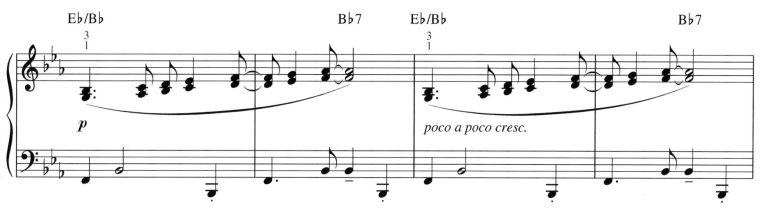

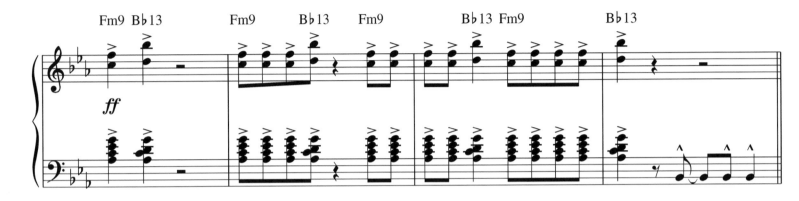

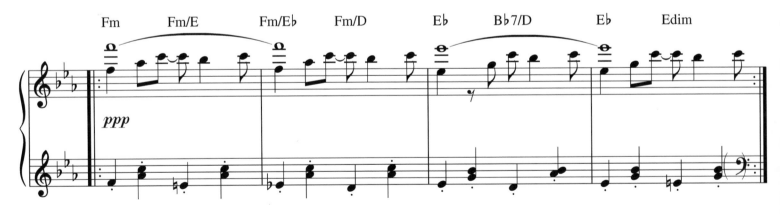

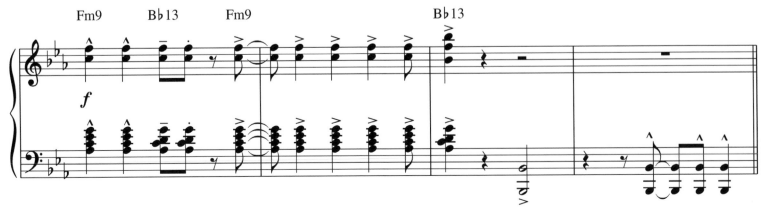

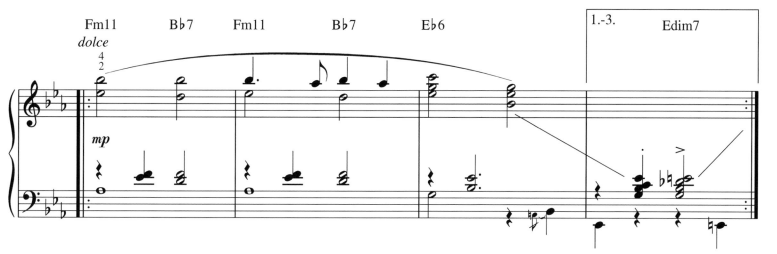
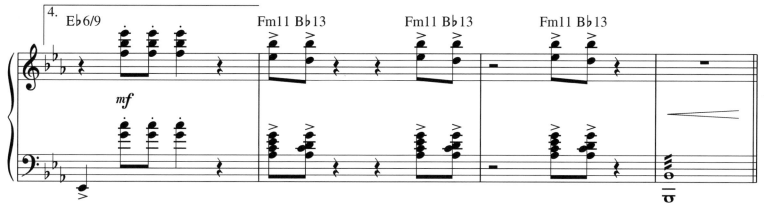

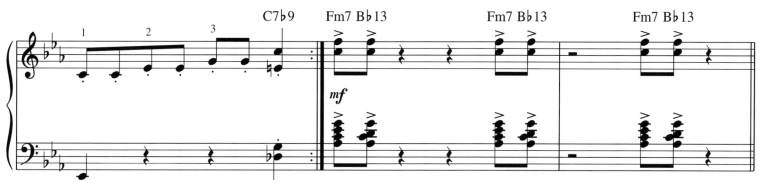

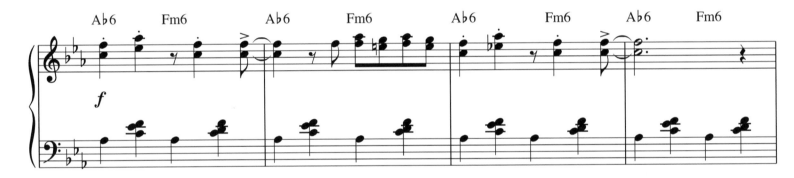

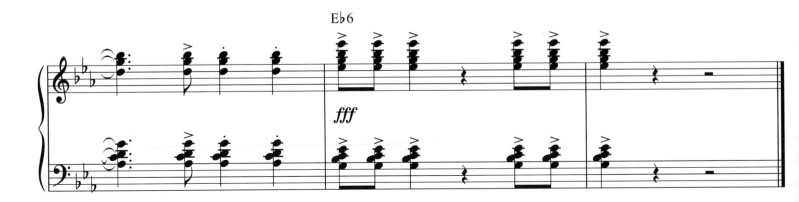

MANTECA

By DIZZY GILLESPIE, WALTER GIL FULLER
and LUCIANO POZO GONZALES

Moderate Latin

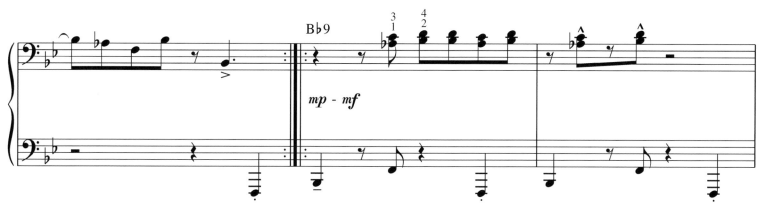

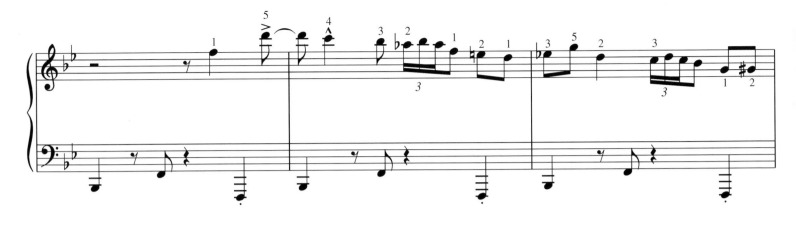

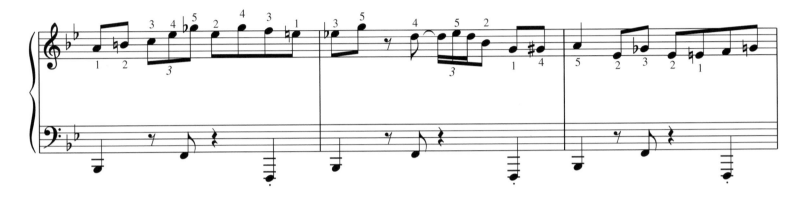

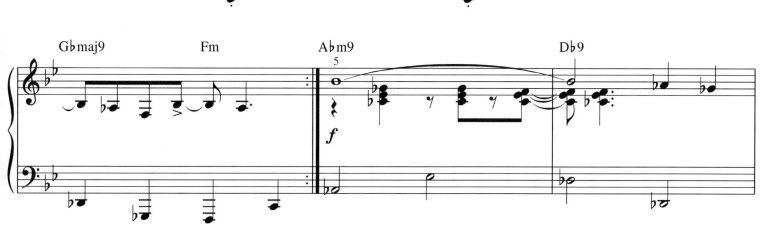

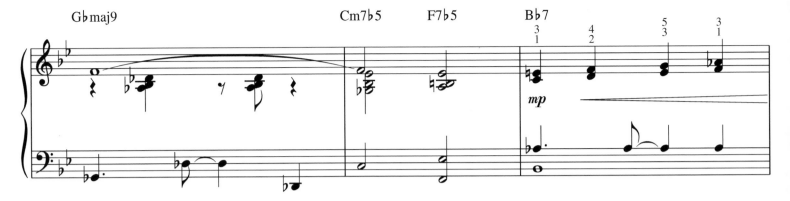

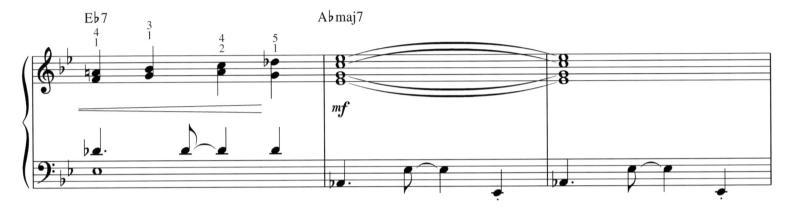

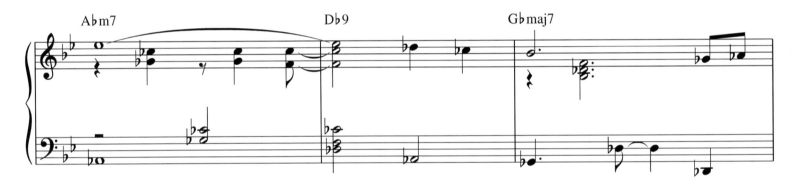

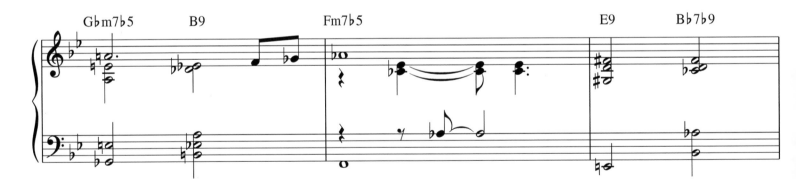

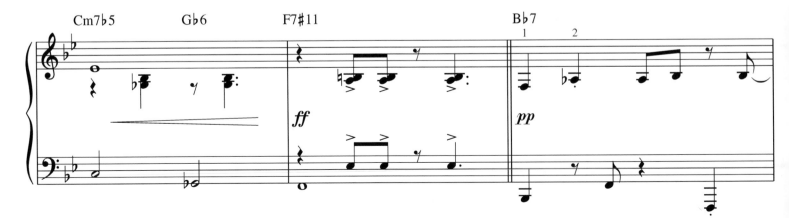

Bb7/Ab

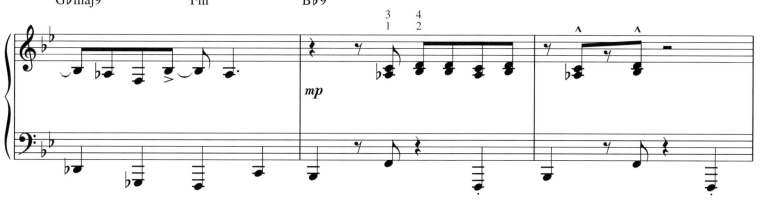

cresc.

Gbmaj9   Fm   Bb9

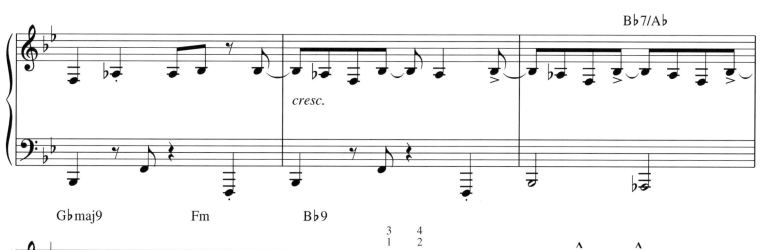

mp

cresc.

ff

8vb

MAS QUE NADA

Words and Music by
JORGE BEN

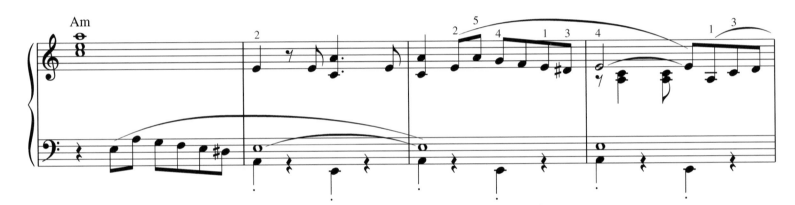

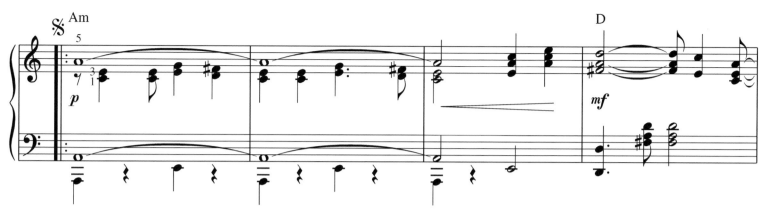

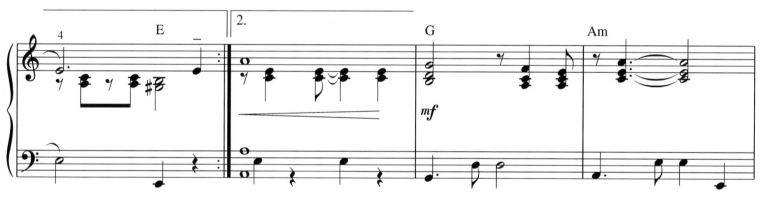

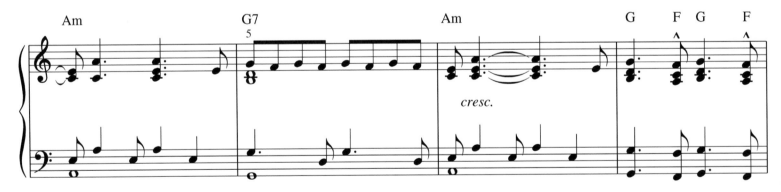

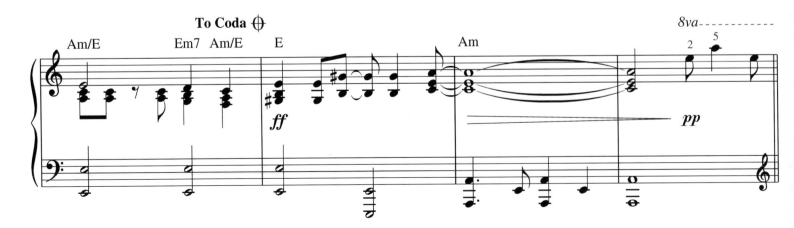

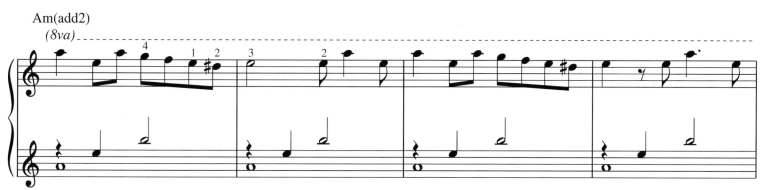

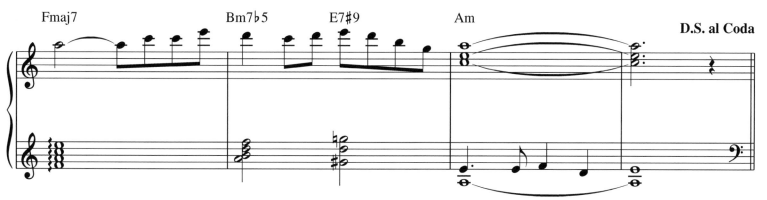

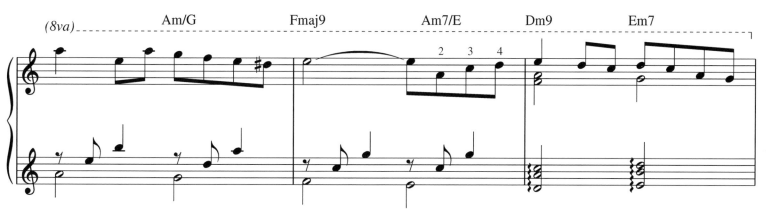

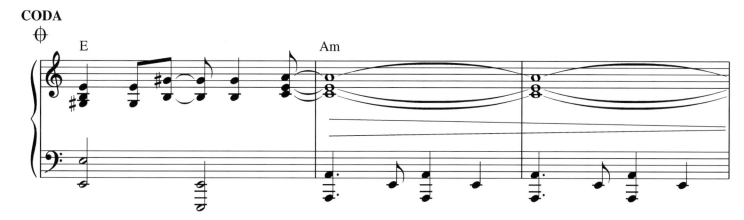

ONCE I LOVED
(Amor em Paz)
(Love in Peace)

Music by ANTONIO CARLOS JOBIM
Portuguese Lyrics by VINICIUS DE MORAES
English Lyrics by RAY GILBERT

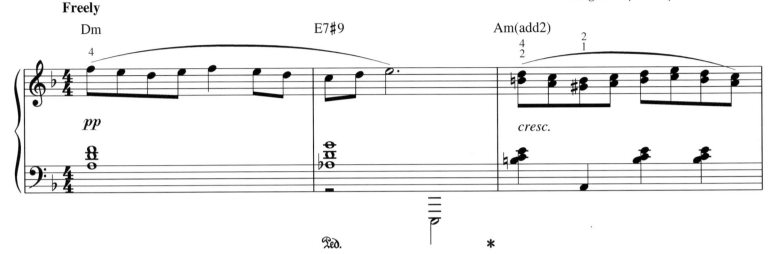

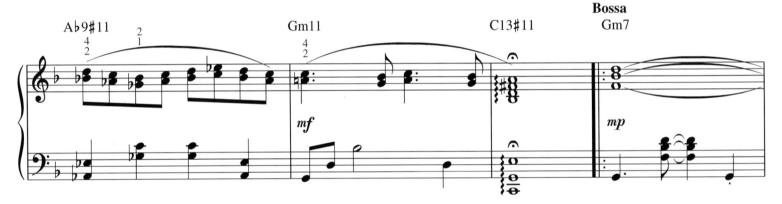

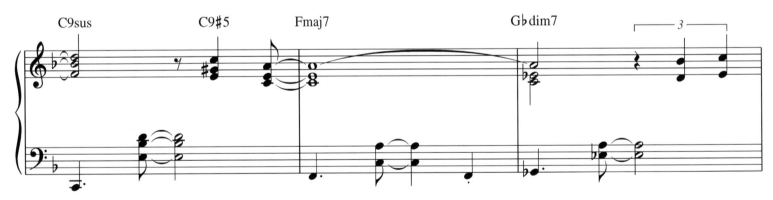

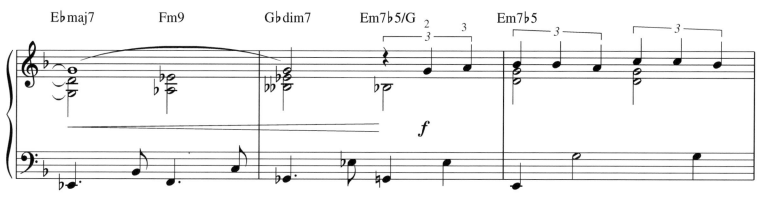

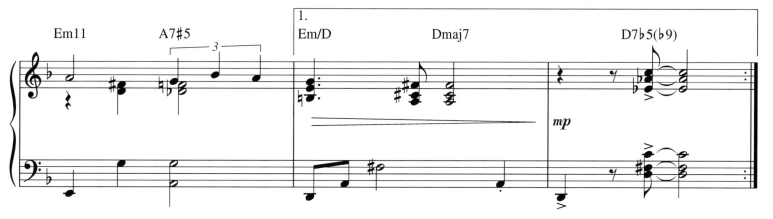

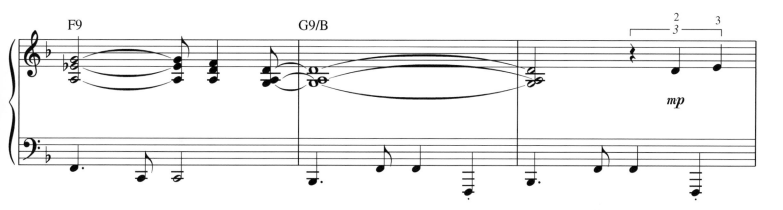

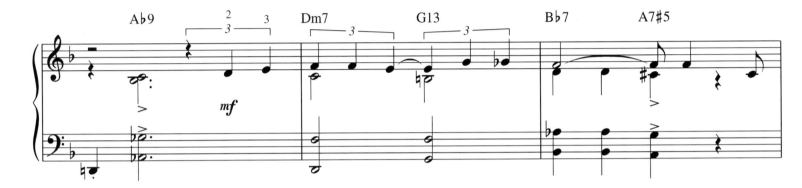

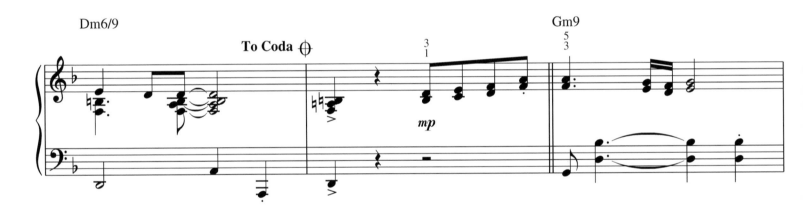

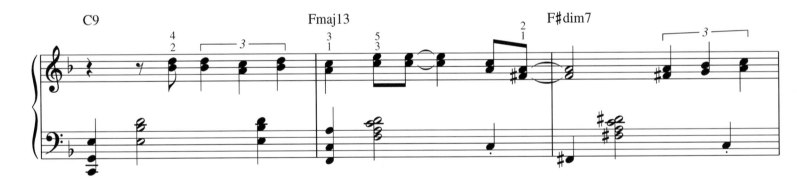

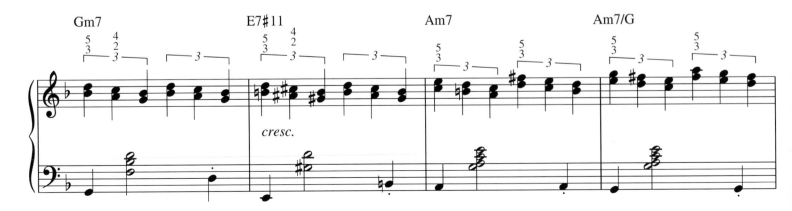

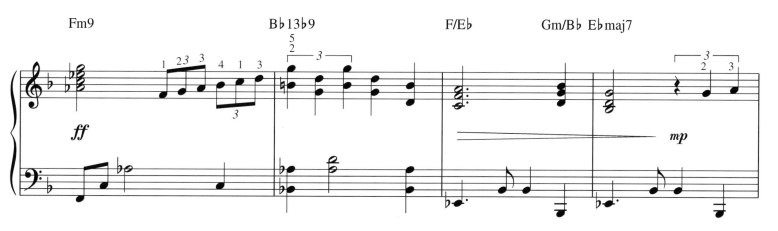

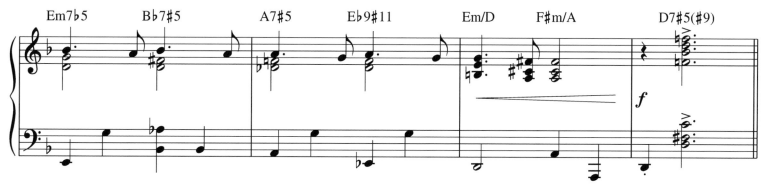

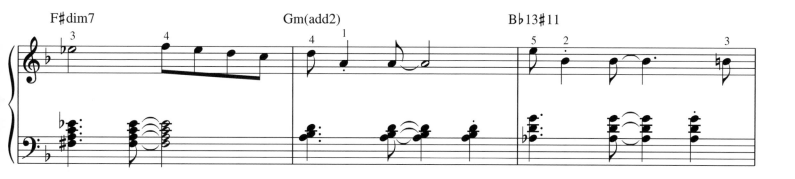

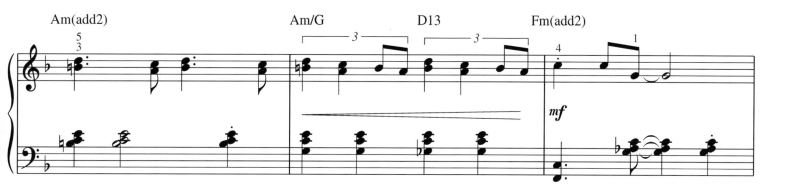

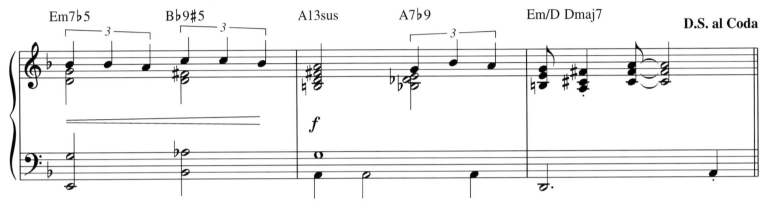

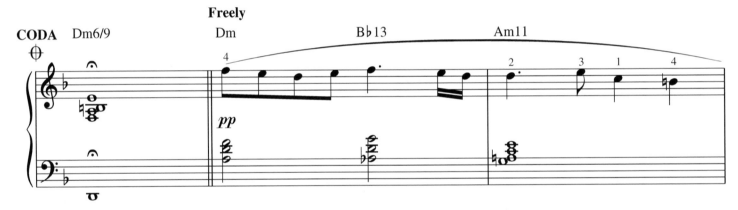

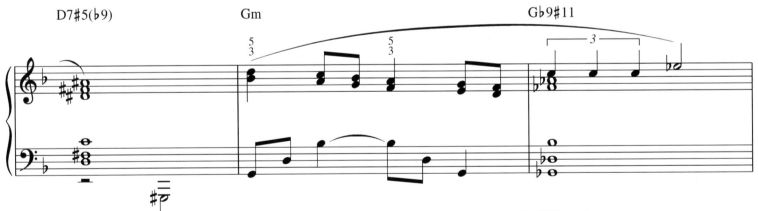

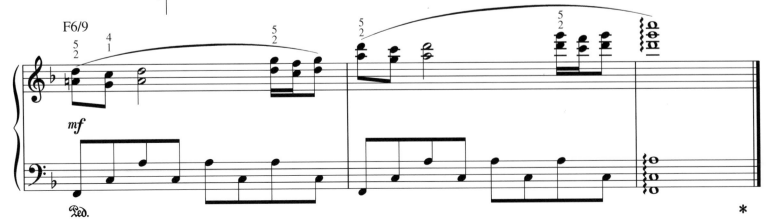

SO NICE
(Summer Samba)

Original Words and Music by MARCOS VALLE
and PAULO SERGIO VALLE
English Words by NORMAN GIMBEL

Medium Bossa Nova

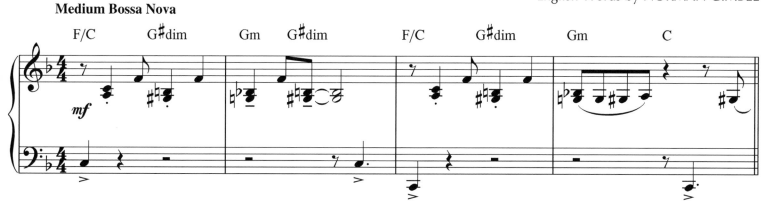

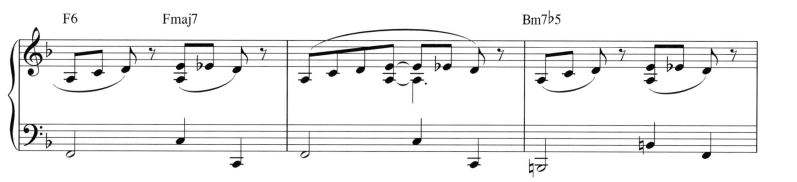

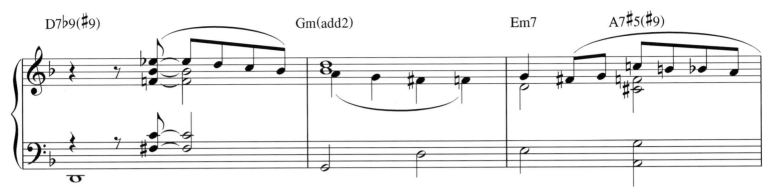

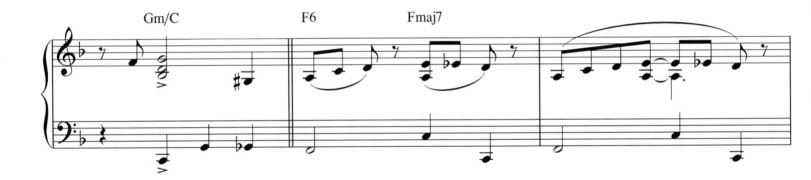

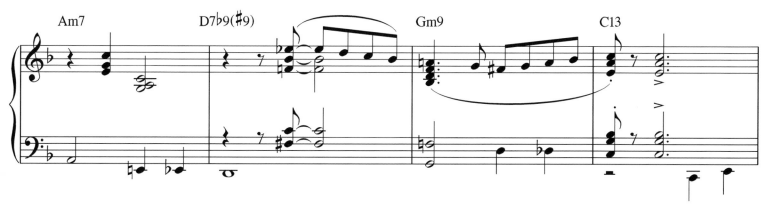

PERFIDIA

Words and Music by
ALBERTO DOMINGUEZ

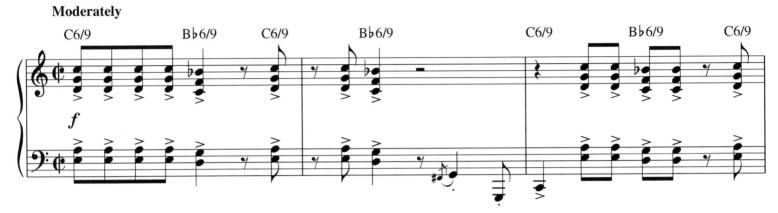

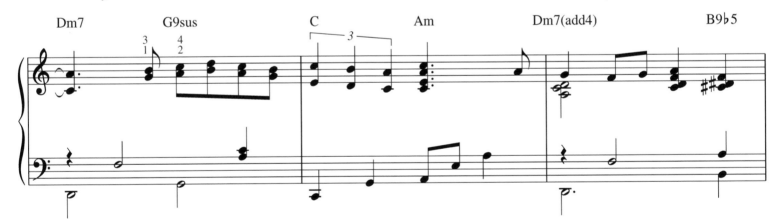

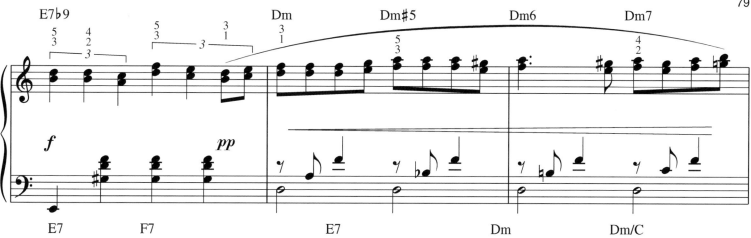

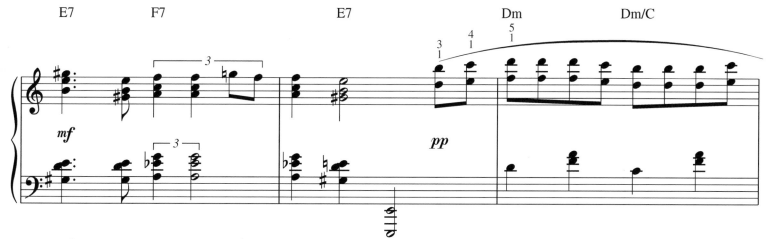

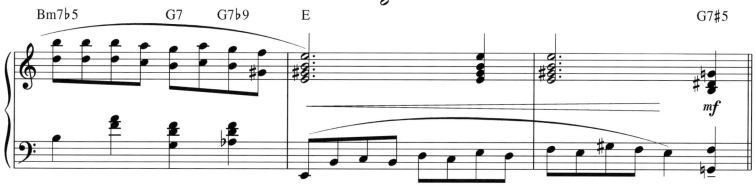

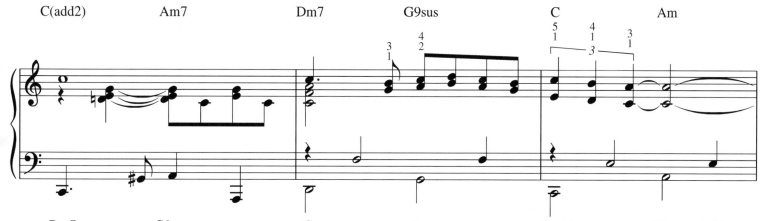

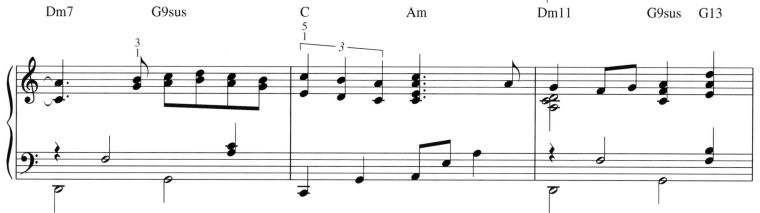

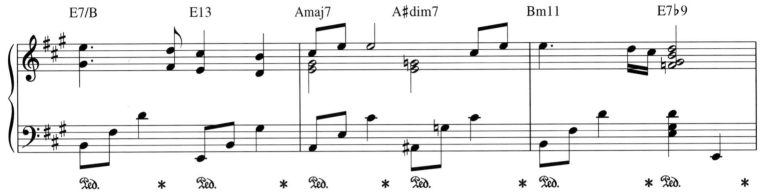

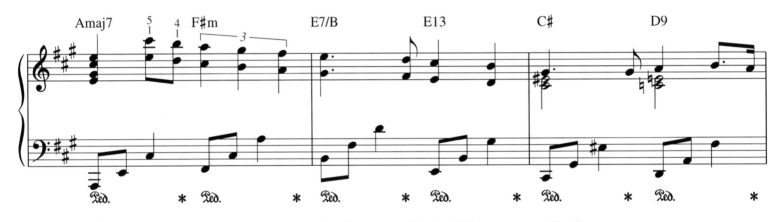

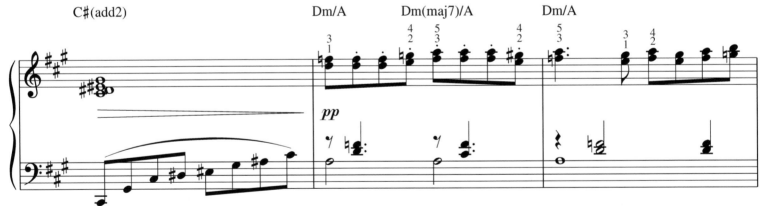

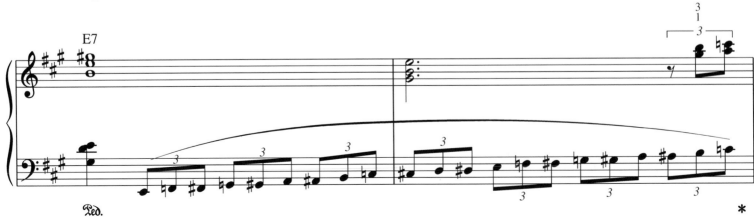

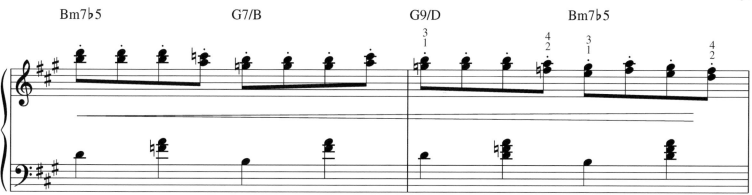

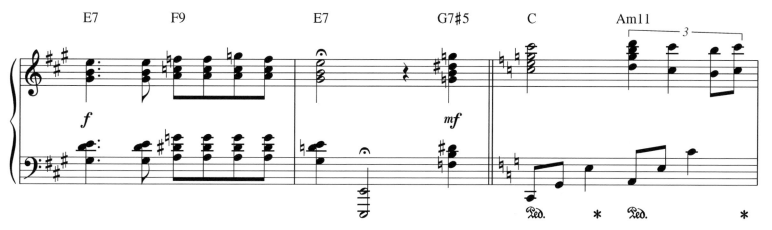

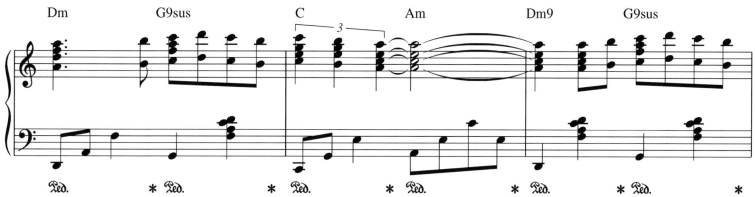

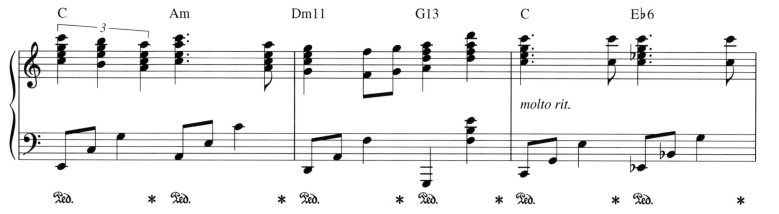

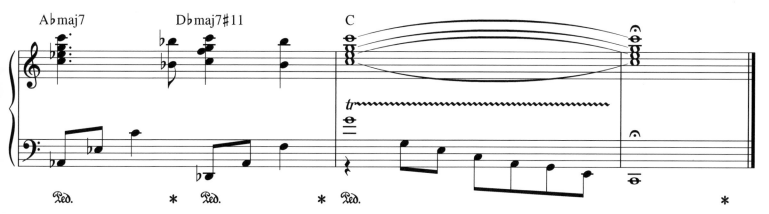

SAMBA DE ORFEU

Words by ANTONIO MARIA
Music by LUIZ BONFA

Moderate Samba

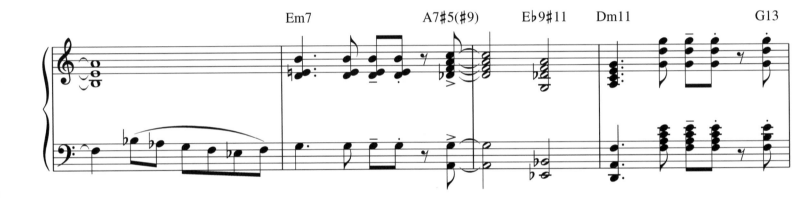

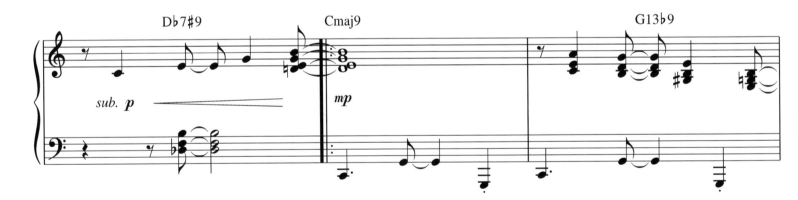

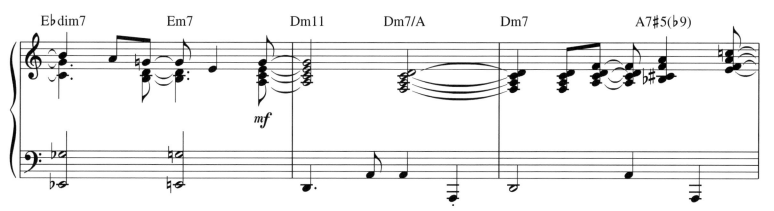

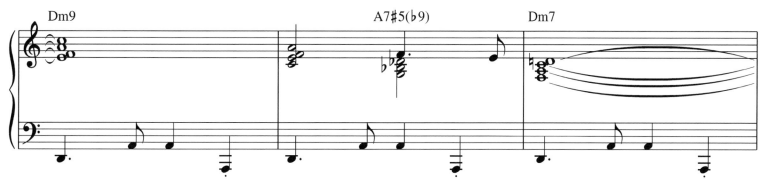

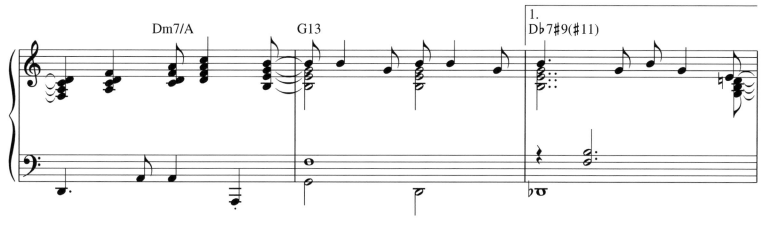

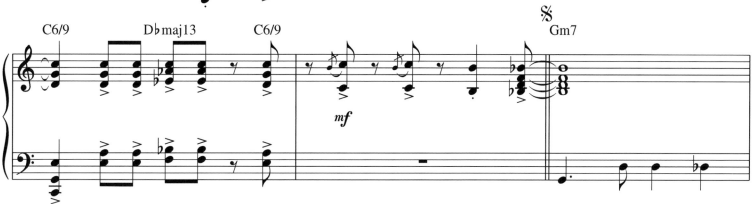

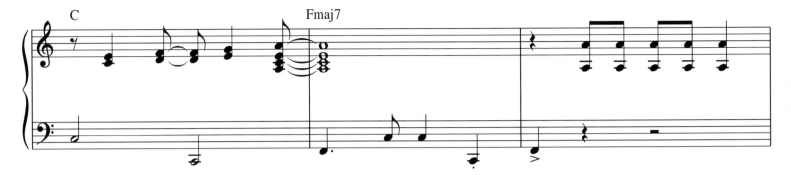

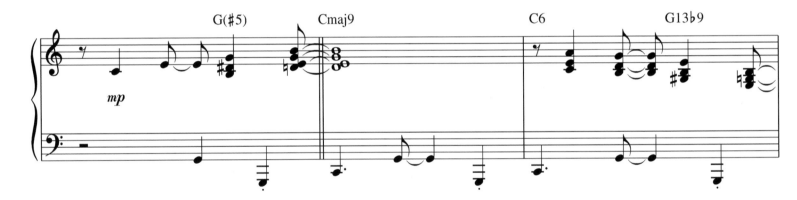

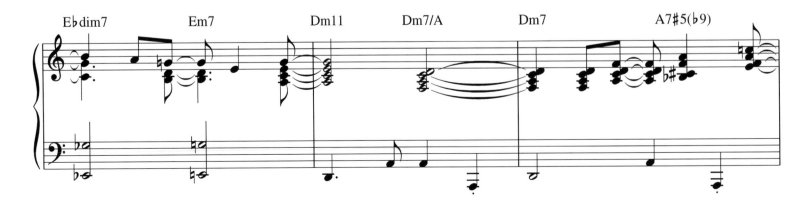

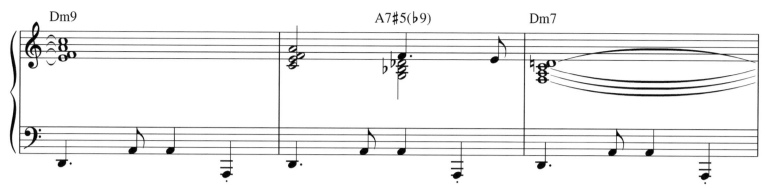

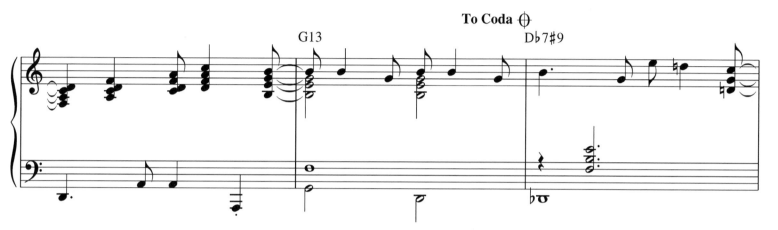

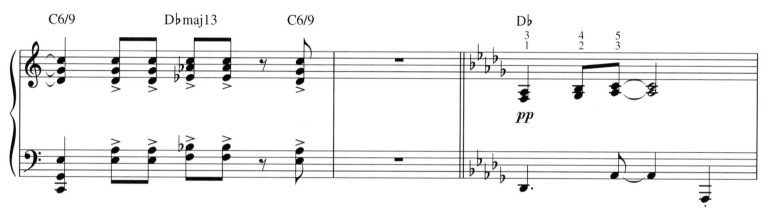

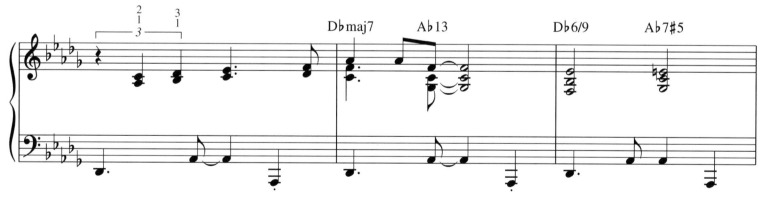

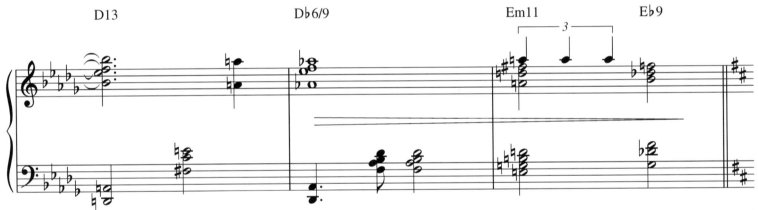

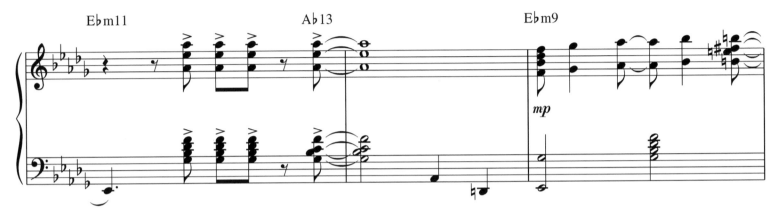

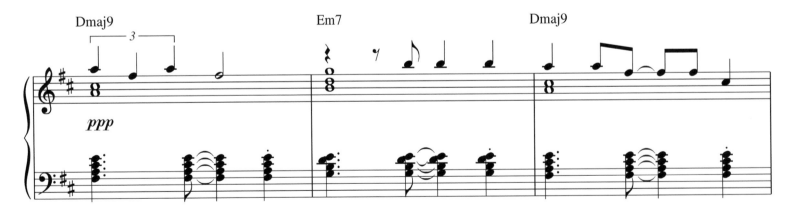

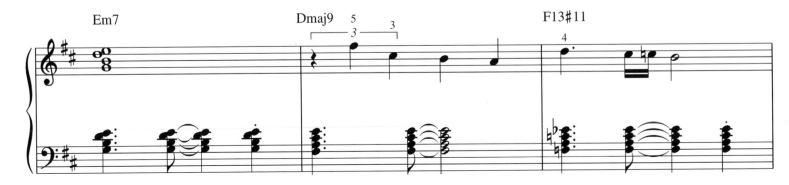

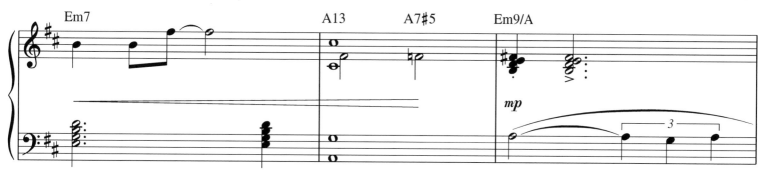

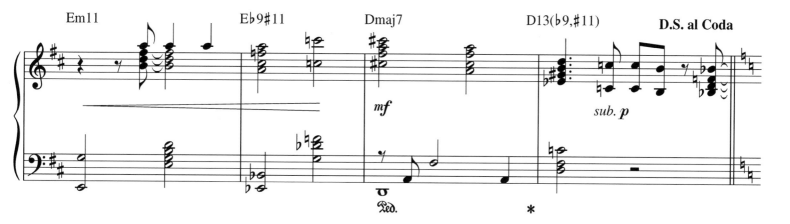

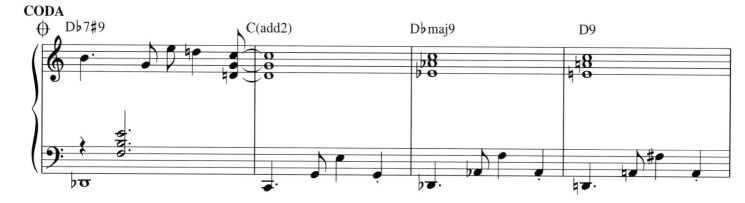

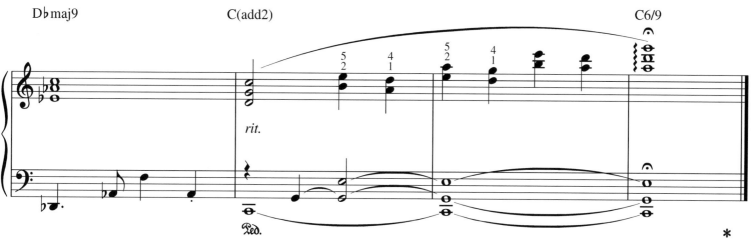

YOU BELONG TO MY HEART
(Solamente Una Vez)

Words and Music by
AGUSTIN LARA

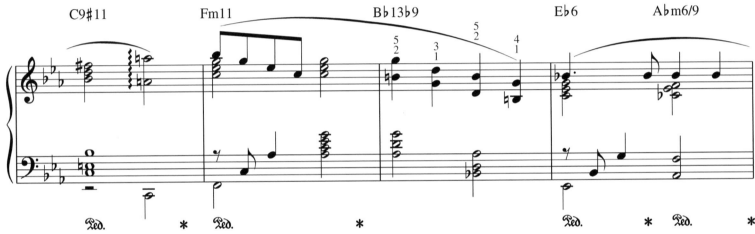

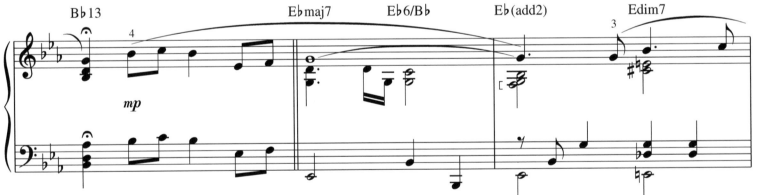

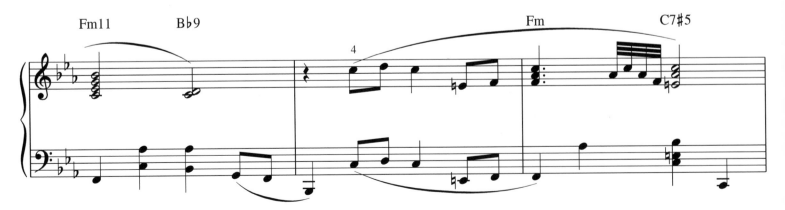

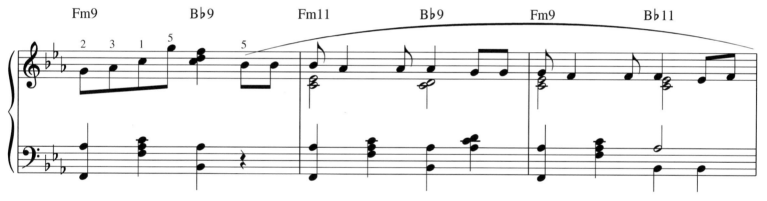

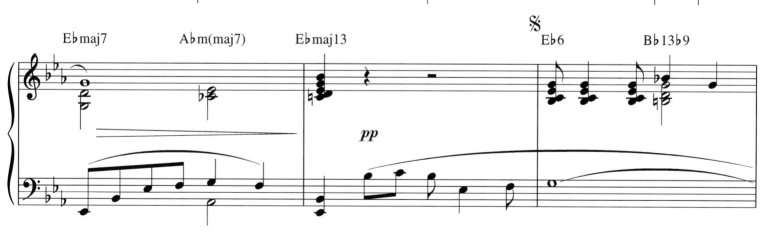

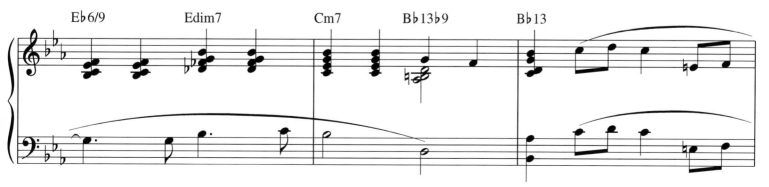

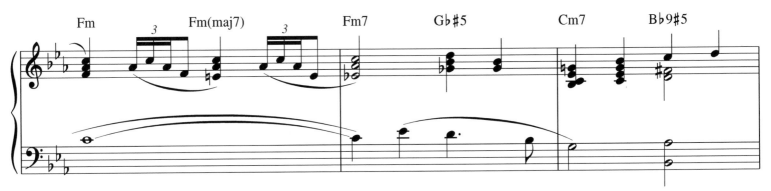

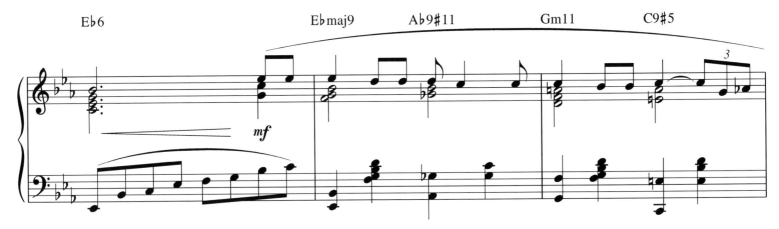

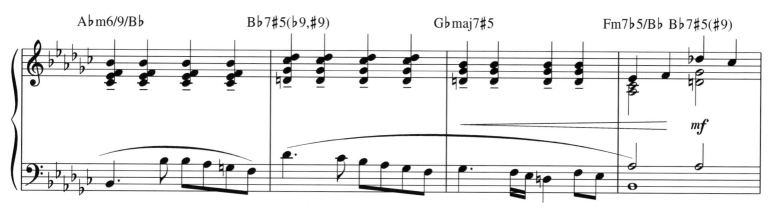

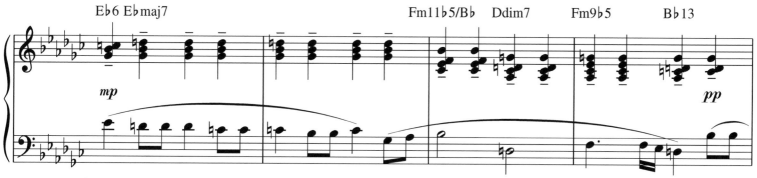

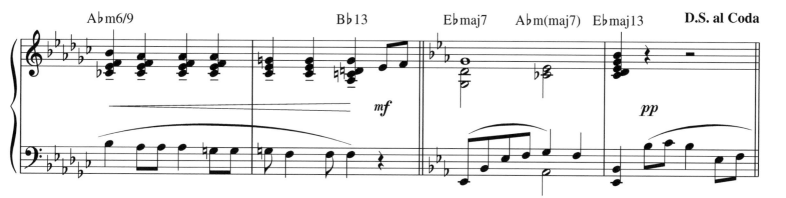

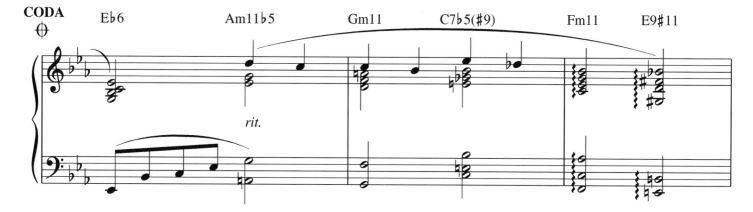

TRISTE

By ANTONIO CARLOS JOBIM

Moderately slow Bossa

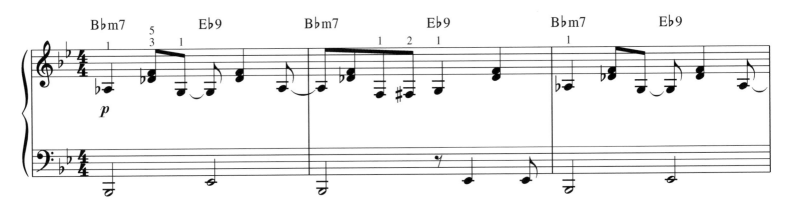

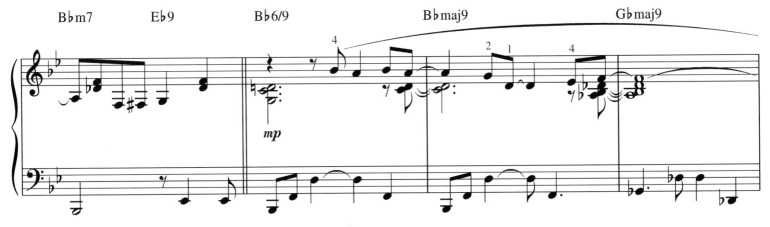

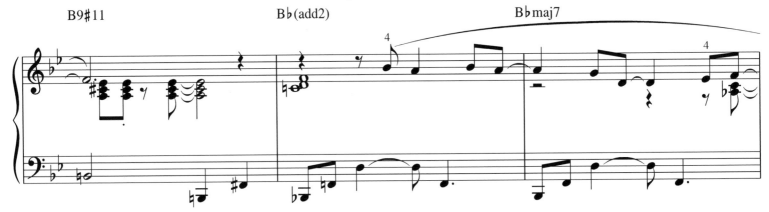

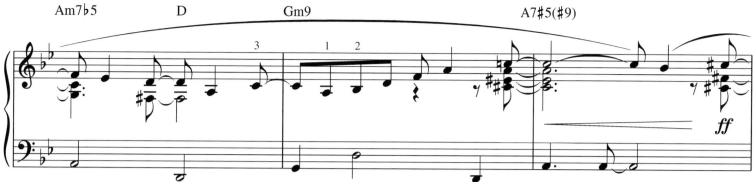

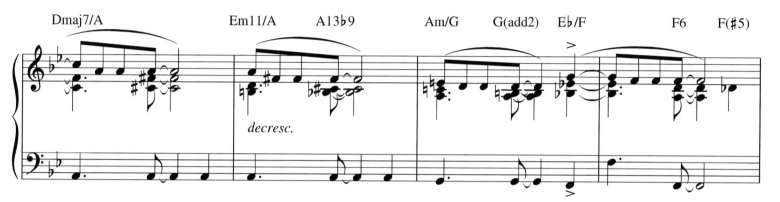

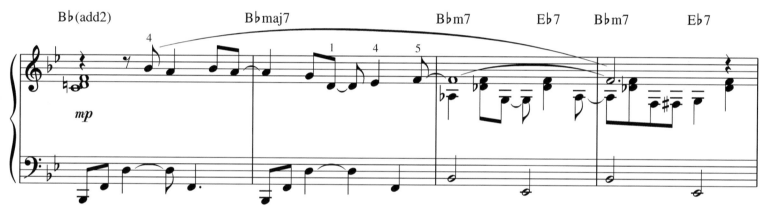

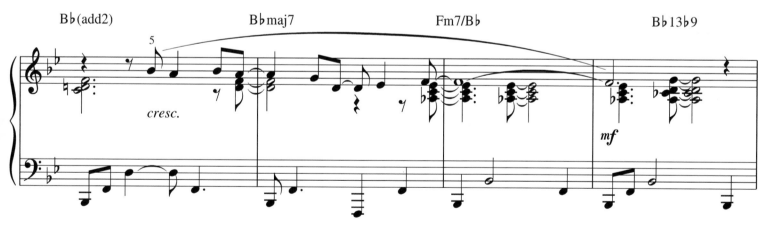

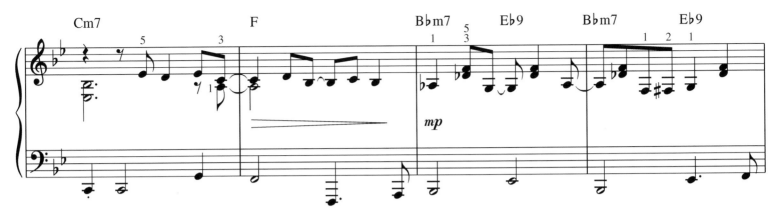

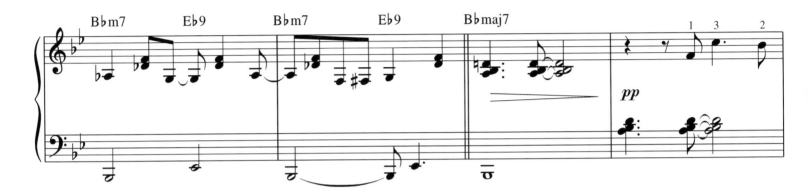

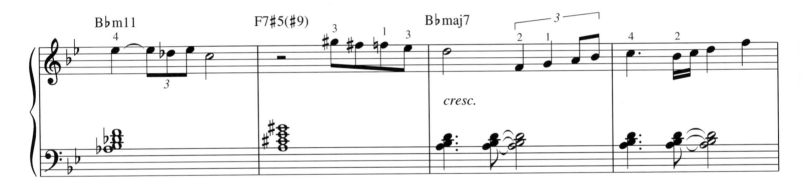

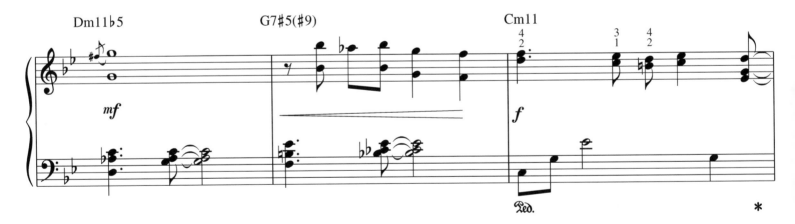

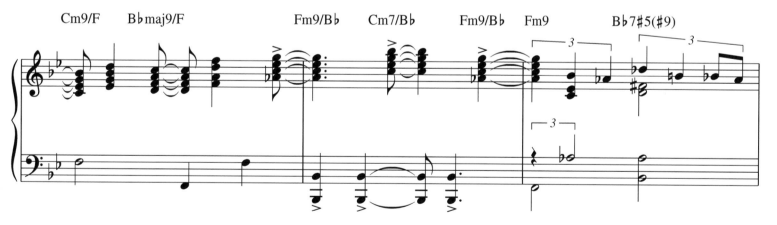

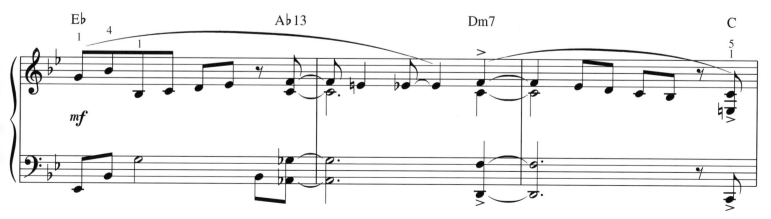

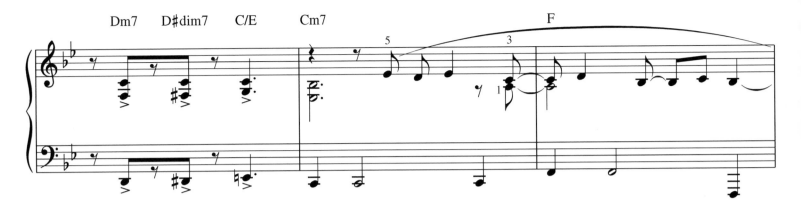

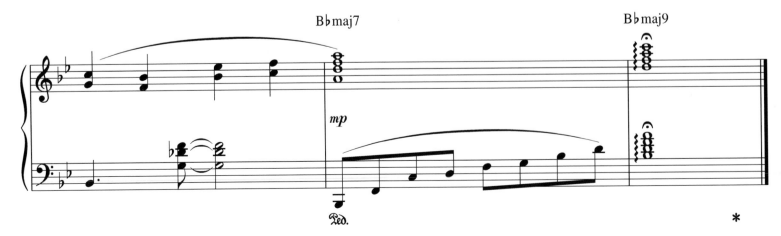